"Nothing changes the way we relate to [...] how God relates to us. Knowing how [...] loves us and forgives us and is gracious and merciful toward us and forbears with us inevitably affects the way we think about other people. My good friend Jessica Thompson has written a book that articulates who God is for us and then shows how that changes the way we are toward others. Thank you, Jessica, for reminding me that God always meets my mess with his mercy and my failure with his forgiveness. Knowing this makes me want to love God and others."

—Tullian Tchividjian, founder of Liberate and author of *One Way Love: Inexhaustible Grace for an Exhausted World*

"We need grace in all our relationships. So much loneliness, feeling betrayed, alienation, anger, vengeance, sadness, grief find their roots in relational conflict. Jessica humbly guides us to see that only by being a recipient of God's grace can we be agents of grace in our relationships. She does this with humor, honesty, and confession from her own experience, not with advice as a relational guru."

—Justin S. Holcomb, Episcopal priest, seminary professor, and author of *On the Grace of God*

"*Everyday Grace* is for all who have struggled to accept their children and honor their parents and initiate with their neighbors and forgive their spouses and respect their bosses and celebrate their rivals. But it is not filled with practical tips that would trivialize the difficulty of these things. Nor is it a book of relational psychology that would strategize a resolution to these things. Instead, it is filled with the Scriptures that speak to these things—helping us to rest in Christ's covering of all our relational failure and inviting us to change by the power of the Holy Spirit."

—Nancy Guthrie, Bible teacher and author

"Relational paradise was lost when our first parents fell into sin. Our desire for change in this area is anywhere between cautiously optimistic and downright cynical. What I enjoy about *Everyday Grace* is that Thompson simply cannot get over the one hope for true reconciliation: God, in Christ, has befriended us."

—Gloria Furman, author of *Glimpses of Grace*
and *Treasuring Christ When Your Hands Are Full*

"Relationships are hard. We know this. Jessica Thompson knows this too and shares how she fights to take her gaze off herself and onto the only one who can help our broken relationships—Jesus. Her method doesn't come from a list of ways to implement change; rather, she focuses on the gospel that transforms hearts and minds. Be encouraged by the good news as you read *Everyday Grace*, for it is the gospel that is our only Hope for our relationship problem."

—Trillia Newbell, author of *Fear and Faith: Finding the Peace
Your Heart Craves* and *United: Captured
by God's Vision for Diversity*

Everyday Grace

INFUSING ALL YOUR RELATIONSHIPS
WITH THE LOVE OF JESUS

JESSICA THOMPSON

BETHANY HOUSE PUBLISHERS
a division of Baker Publishing Group
Minneapolis, Minnesota

© 2015 by Jessica Thompson

Published by Bethany House Publishers
11400 Hampshire Avenue South
Bloomington, Minnesota 55438
www.bethanyhouse.com

Bethany House Publishers is a division of
Baker Publishing Group, Grand Rapids, Michigan

Printed in the United States of America

Library of Congress Cataloging-in-Publication Data
Thompson, Jessica.
    Everyday grace : infusing all your relationships with the love of Jesus / Jessica Thompson.
        pages cm
    Includes bibliographical references.
    Summary: "Using a biblical approach to navigate interactions with others, the author encourages readers to give and receive grace in every relationship"—Provided by publisher.
        ISBN 978-0-7642-1299-4 (pbk. : alk. paper) 1. Interpersonal relations—Religious aspects—Christianity. 2. Love—Religious aspects—Christianity. 3. Grace (Theology) I. Title.
    BV4597.52.T465 2015
    248'4—dc23   2014041511

Cover design by Jennifer Parker

Author is represented by Wolgemuth and Associates.

To my Cody

Your commitment to love me through it all is astounding.
You reflect the way Christ loves the church. I love you.

Contents

Foreword

If there's one commodity in this world that's rare, it's got to be grace. Let's face it, we all live in a quid pro quo world, a world in which we're taught to believe that "what goes around comes around." We're entranced by "pay it forward" scenarios, hoping that perhaps in the future someone will pay it forward for us.

Although these sayings seem modern, the truth is that they aren't; in fact, they've been with us since Adam and Eve first believed the lie that they should trample on each other as a way to achieve godhood. And when they did that, they not only turned our thinking on its head but also turned us in on ourselves, a condition Martin Luther described five hundred years ago with the Latin phrase *incurvatus in se*. Yes, even then, men and women, boys and girls were self-focused, curved in on themselves, and chained to the belief that their desires were ultimate and that all of their relationships, with both God and man, exist primarily to satiate their craving for preeminence. We're no different. So we construct self-focused ways to motivate people to live as they should. But this kind of living isn't for God or even for our neighbor; it's primarily for ourselves, so that we can demand from others what we want and approve of ourselves at the end of the day.

It's into this desperate world that God speaks the word *grace*. Rather than repaying us as our sins deserve, he poured out all his wrath on his perfect Son and granted to us all the blessings he had earned in a life of complete faith and love. Traditionally, grace has been defined as "God's riches at Christ's expense," and it is that. We get his riches. He gets our wrath. Nothing in Christ's life or death has anything at all to do with quid pro quo. Certainly what went around from him didn't come to him . . . at least not before the resurrection. If there was ever any man who was not curved in on himself it was Jesus. And yet, because of grace, he agreed to pay it forward to us even as he cried in agony on Golgotha's mount.

And this grace, this amazing commodity, is the only medicine powerful enough to turn us away from ourselves and toward others. It is only by grace that we will experience the renewal and resurrection of our relationships. It is only as we see how we've been loved and welcomed despite our sin that we are able to love and welcome other sinners.

Of course, there are plenty of books out there that tell you how you should pay it forward so that you can get what you want from your relationships. But these schemes will ultimately leave you empty because you'll still be the same old *incurvatus in se* you and you'll wonder why no one else is working as hard as you are while watching the whole thing come crumbling down under the weight of your demandingness. It's simply impossible to be freed from measuring how others are responding to our love when we live under the creed of "what goes around comes around." You don't need steps to better relationships or rungs on a ladder, you need a Rescuer. And, gloriously, that's just what you've been given.

So it is with great joy that I recommend this book to you. Of course, I could tell you to read this book because my dear daughter and dear friend, Jessica, wrote it, and I'm her mom. I could tell you to read this because I have watched her life and have seen it overflow with grace time and time again with her family, her friends, her church . . . yes, even with her mom. But I'm not telling you to read this book because I love Jessica; I'm telling you to read it because she gets grace and how it plays out in our relationships and that it is only the deep, sweet, refreshing, mind-boggling truth of God's grace that will enable and empower you to love your neighbor as yourself. She knows that all of our schemes to be loved are forever swallowed up in this truth: *Jesus loves me, this I know.*

So, let that precious reality infect and inform all your thoughts, and soon, without noticing it, you'll become kinder and more loving. Why? Because you've been loved. This is the message you'll find here . . . and I'm so happy about it.

—Elyse Fitzpatrick

Acknowledgments

*M*y mind is weak. I sit down to write these acknowledgments fully aware that I am going to forget some very key people. So if you are reading this hoping to see your name and it isn't here, I am sorry. I have had too much chocolate today and not enough brain food and other various excuses.

Thank you to Erik Wolgemuth. This would not have happened without your continual input and encouragement. You are more than my agent; you are a dear friend and a trusted mentor of sorts. Thank you for putting up with me and my silliness and my horrible grammar.

Thank you to my husband. From fifteen to forty you have been the one who has known the worst about me and continued to love me. I am grateful for you, beyond words.

Thank you to my family. Mom, we are beyond blessed to share all that we share. You are my mom, teacher, mentor, friend, hero, fellow traveler, and co-worker; I love you. Dad, your faithfulness and commitment to always love is inspiring. To my brothers, James and Joel, . . . J3 4evah.

Thank you to my kids, Wes, Hayden, and Allie. Thank you for loving me. You teach me every single day what grace and kindness look like.

Thank you to my church family, Westview Church. To my pastor, Jesse, and his fabulous wife, Angie, you guys are the best. To my gospel community, Mark, Keri, Katie, Anthony, Kelley, Wayne, and Kei, thank you for your prayers. You all support me in such practical and beautiful ways. I love you.

Thank you to all those who teach me through their writing: Jami Nato, Lore Ferguson, Gloria Furman, Trillia Newbell, Sammy Rhodes, David Zahl, Paul Zahl, Scotty Smith, Preston Sprinkle, Nancy Guthrie, Timothy Paul Jones, Daniel Montgomery, Barb Duguid, Hannah Singer, Wayne Houk, the whole She Reads Truth family, Tullian Tchividjian, Steve Brown, Justin Holcomb.

Thank you to my fellow Dropping Keys peeps: Kimm Crandall, Lauren Larkin, Jeff Block, Chad West, and Rachel Cohen. You all just do not stop dispensing the good news—I love it.

Introduction

*A*fter I ran a quick search on Amazon for "Christian Relationship Books," I was stunned to find over twenty thousand results. Over twenty thousand books on relationships from a Christian worldview are for sale right now. This is a staggering number—and, yes, I realize I am just adding to it—but let me tell you why this book will be different from the majority of books out there on relationships. I don't have a bunch of great advice. Now, before you start wondering, *Why in the world did I buy this book?* let me tell you why I think this is good news. It's good because as Christians, we don't *need* any more relationship advice! Those twenty thousand "Christian Relationship Books" can give you advice on how to be a better wife, mother, daughter, friend, employee, and so on. There are experts from every field who can tell you exactly how to maximize your influence, or build a legacy, or make your children excel, or have the best marriage on the block. Those might all be fine and may actually work—for a time.

The problem, however, is that while *you* may be following all of the right steps to a better relationship, it doesn't mean your spouse or your friend is. And if we're honest with ourselves, how many of us can even follow all the right steps in any book? For the most part, we know what to do in relationships: Be loving, give unselfishly, don't get angry . . . and on and on. And yet, here you find yourself reading another book (and me writing it!) on how to have better relationships. Why is there such a breakdown? If we all want good relationships, and generally speaking we have a pretty good idea of what to do in a relationship, why is there so much brokenness?

The point of this book is not to give you a push in the right direction. We need more than a push. We need to be made *alive*. My hope is that this book will bring life to your soul. But first, we have to diagnose the real problem.

Since I am a woman, I will be primarily addressing women in this book. But we all know that relationship difficulties are not strictly a female problem. They are a human problem. So occasionally I will also talk to the men who might be reading or listening. I would encourage my female readers to share and discuss these thoughts with the men in their lives as well, or invite them to read the book for themselves.

Lastly, I need to say at the outset that I don't have all my relationships perfectly together. I experience brokenness just like every single person reading this book. My goal is to be brutally honest with you about my own relationships. I don't want you to think for one minute that I am a relationship expert, because I am not. I wholeheartedly agree with Martin Luther and say about myself that "I am just one beggar telling another beggar where to find bread."

The Problem
With Us

*J*anet Jackson had a pop hit in the '80s that sums up how most of us view our relationships. The chorus repeats over and over, "What have you done for me lately?" She asks this question because the answer provides her relational guidelines. That is, for Ms. Jackson (and often for you and me, if we're honest), "You do for me, I will do for you" is the religion of the day. You be a good husband to me, I will be a good wife to you. You be a faithful friend to me, I will be a faithful friend to you. You preach the way I like it and appreciate my gifts, I will stay at your church. You be a good father or mother, I will be a respectful child. You be a good child, I will be a nice mother. If you don't do what you are supposed to do, then that releases me from my obligation to love you, and I can do whatever I want to do. This mind-set is not just a sign of our own times, of course. It was been around a long time and was at one time referred to as "Ka me, ka thee." *Ka* means "to serve." You serve me, I will serve you. Sir Walter Scott, a nineteenth-century Scottish

19

novelist and poet, once wrote, "Ka me, ka thee, is the proverb all over the world."

"What have you done for me lately?" I often feel that if I am not looking out for myself and my interests, no one will. And while Janet Jackson describes how we feel toward each other, the intro to the TV show *My Name Is Earl* describes how we feel toward God. In this intro, Earl gives a monologue saying that he was a terrible person. He describes how whenever something good happened to him, something bad would immediately follow. He calls this *karma*. He says he finally learned his lesson and decided to make a change in his life. He concludes, "So I made a list of everything bad I've ever done and one by one I'm gonna make up for all my mistakes. I'm just trying to be a better person."

We often live with God by the rule of karma, as Earl defines it,[1] trying to make up for all the wrongs we have done. I think if I can just make up for it, if I can just do better, then God will take care of my needs, all the while forgetting that he has actually already taken care of every need I truly have. This question of "What have you done for me lately?" in relationship is a sure lack of belief that God is faithful and will provide all that I need. I think if I do my part and work hard, everybody else had better do their part and work hard too. I can't leave it up to God. I must take care of things myself. The problem with this thinking is that in reality I don't really work hard at my relationships. So often I am self-focused, worried about my own needs and desires, instead of being "genuinely concerned" for the welfare of others (Philippians 2:20).

An attitude of "you give to me because I give to you" is terribly exhausting. First of all, I never live up to my own expectations. I am never really the friend, spouse, parent that I want others to be. This results in a pulling up of the bootstraps and trying harder. Second, not only do I fail, others fail me. So if I am looking to others for my own happiness, satisfaction, security, or acceptance, I will constantly be disappointed and angry. Truly my only source of joy can be my God, who never disappoints me and is the only one who perfectly relates.

With this mind-set, you and I go trudging through everyday relationships. And yet we long for something else. We long for a love that gives its all to us. We are taught very early through childhood fairy tales that there is that special someone out there just for you, and he or she will change your entire life. They will love you regardless of what you do or don't do. In fact, as soon as they see you, they will know you are the one for them. As we grow up, we find that this idealistic relationship isn't really out there . . . or maybe we just haven't found it yet. So we go to romance novels, soap operas, or romantic movies and look there for the love we want. We see it portrayed on the screen, or on the pages of the book we are reading, or in the lyrics to our favorite song, and we can't understand why we can't have that same love. We start to redouble our efforts with our loved ones. We go back to our *ka me, ka thee* ideal and think, "If I just work harder at being a better (you fill in the blank), they will be better too. If I do more, I will get more back."

The truth is we don't want *ka me, ka thee* or *karma*, even though we think we do. The gospel refutes this idea completely. It is anti-karma and pro-grace. The gospel says that even though you aren't good enough now and actually never will be good enough in your own good works, I am going to give to you anyway. The gospel tells us that all we have earned has been given to the Son and all the Son has earned has been given undeservingly to us. If we try to rely on karma to see us through, it will be an endless life of working never to obtain. If we rest our souls in the gospel, our lives will be full of receiving, even though we could never work hard enough to receive the gift we have been given.

Our reality is one of brokenness. Our reality is one where we fight with our parents, yet still long for a safe place to call home. Our reality is that we are sinfully impatient and angry with our kids when they don't get in the car quickly enough, and then we feel guilty for the way we've treated them. Our reality is that we are jealous of our friends for their other friendships, and yet hate that we feel that way. Our reality is that we are angry and demanding with our spouses, all the while wondering why we can't love and be loved the way we have seen in books, movies, and TV.

Recently, I have heard from two different friends who are experiencing hurt in a relationship. One is feeling unappreciated by a dear friend to whom she has given so much. At the same time, she also feels guilty that maybe she isn't doing enough for this friend. The guilt she is feeling has convinced her that since she hasn't done enough, her friend doesn't appreciate her. The other friend is dealing with deep and complicated feelings of hurt and confusion toward her parents. She grew up with an abusive father and a mother who enabled him and didn't defend her children. Yet my friend still tried to repair the relationship. Even so, her parents dismissed her attempts and severed the relationship even further by denial, and then in turn accused her of not being the daughter she should be.

We each have our own stories like the two above. We all have tales of broken relationships. I am sure most of us can think of at least one relationship that we feel regret over. We wish things could have been different or could be different now. What is our hope? What is our help? How can we, as sinners, live with and love other sinners?

Our increasingly self-centered society tells us to love only those who are worthy, those who earn our love, those who prove themselves. And likewise, we are only worthy to be loved if we have proven ourselves. Most people in our modern world hum along with Janet Jackson and nod their heads in agreement with Earl: *I will do better, be a better friend, and surely they will be better and God will bless me.* The gospel obliterates both of these ideas. Concerning relationship, the gospel says:

> For while we were still weak, at the right time Christ died for the ungodly. For one will scarcely die for a righteous person—though perhaps for a good person one would dare even to die—but God shows his love for us in that while we were still sinners, Christ died for us.
>
> Romans 5:6–8

How radically life-changing would it be to live in the truth of this freedom every day? How life-changing would it be for your relationships if you didn't live with crushing expectations hanging over your loved ones' heads?

All of us know the white-hot gaze of a loved one we have disappointed. My siblings and I used to call that specific look from our mother the "Fish-Eye." (*Uh-oh, Mom's giving you the Fish-Eye. . . . You better knock that off or Mom will give you the Fish-Eye. . . .*) There's a good reason for this odd name—think about when a dead fish is floating on the water and there's that one eye fixed on you in an unrelenting gaze, asking, *Why didn't you feed me today or* all last week? Or, *Why did you think it would be fun to dump the entire bottle of fish food in this tank, huh?* I myself have perfected this look with my own children. I don't have to say a single word and they can feel my disappointment. Oh, for a change in my heart that I would be able to see their sin and give a look of grace instead—a look of understanding.

When you and I can come to the depths of our sinfulness without trying to cover ourselves, without thinking that God is looking at us with a disappointed gaze, that is when we will be able to love without any thought of ourselves at all. We are a performance-based people, which is completely ironic, because our performance every day is far less than perfect. We live in performance-based relationships. "What have you done for me lately?" You love me and *then* I'll love you. Again, if we could only see the hypocrisy in this, since we don't *ever* love the way we should love. We know this is true, so we hide behind "trying harder," or we avoid the truth by filling our minds and hearts with the numerous ways that others have failed.

There is, however, wonderful hope. We're not doomed to lives full of miserable ka-me-ka-thee-based relationships.

Our hope in relationship is Jesus. Our joy in relationship is remembering how graciously he has loved us. As funny and counterintuitive as this sounds, our relationships cannot be about us; they must be about him. As our gaze turns from how we should be treated to how we've been treated by the One who has every right to cast judgment, then we will know true and intimate fellowship. All of us long for relationships that are fulfilling and loving, but the problem is that we are looking for them in the wrong places. We already have the relationship we all desire. We don't need to use each other anymore to feel loved and wanted; we don't need to look to others to build our self-esteem. We look to Christ alone, who has loved the unlovable, accepted the unacceptable, and given us exactly what we don't deserve. This love will revolutionize our relationships.

The Beatles had it right when they said, "All you need is love." Unfortunately, the love they were talking about was supposed to be found in each other. Beloved, there is no hope in finding the love you desire by looking to each other. You are truly loved unceasingly, unquenchably, and irrevocably now. Let God's love fuel your love for others.

I know this sounds like a utopian idea, spiritual-sounding words that have no *oomph* behind them. Right about now you may be saying, "Great! So what? What exactly do I need to do to let his love fuel me? How does God's love for me in Christ help me to love my brother who is an alcoholic and won't talk to me?" My hope is that while we journey together through this book, you will find that our Savior's love is the only thing that can change the way you relate to others. As you see that Christ calls you his friend (John 15:15), you will be able to love your friends without expectation of finding a perfect friendship because that perfect friend is already yours. You will be able to love those who are outside of your little circle of friends because Jesus loved you even though you were outside of his circle. As a matter of fact, you were his enemy. You will be able to be unselfish with your friends, because your identity doesn't come from who is standing next to you, but rather who has laid down his very life for you. You won't be continually worried about what your friends think of you, because you will have heard and believed his word of grace and acceptance toward you.

As you see that God calls you his bride (Ephesians 5:25–27), you won't look to your earthly spouse to fulfill all your desires to be loved unconditionally, to be known perfectly, and to be dealt with patiently, because you already have all of those things in Christ. He calls you his bride. He loves you as you long to be loved. He knows every intimate detail about you. He prays for you continually. The more your heart steeps in this truth, the freer you will be to love your spouse even when he or she fails you. You won't have to keep a record of their wrongs, because you will remember that Christ has irrevocably canceled your record of wrongs. You will be able to love them when they don't love you back because Christ's love for you never stops, never gives up.

These truths and more are the only solution for our brokenness. Although we won't ever be the perfect friend, spouse, parent, or employee, we can know that we have the perfect Father, Groom, Brother, Friend, and King! Such knowledge will allow us the freedom to love others without thinking, *"What have you done for me lately?"* We will be released to love with only Christ in mind, and this will revolutionize our relationships.

2

The Perfection
of God

The Trinity

When my boys were younger they loved playing with LEGOs. It was always the most anticipated present of Christmas and birthdays. When they were little, they didn't really want to put the pieces together; they just wanted to play with the end result. But as they grew older that changed. The enjoyment came just as much from putting it together as it did from playing with their new spaceship or castle or house. To me the beauty of LEGOs has always been that you get to watch the process from the beginning—just some random pieces in different bags—to the end—what it was always intended to be. So it is with relationship. We need to go back to the very first relationship, the very beginning, in order to watch the loveliness of relationship unfold. We will not only see what a perfect relationship looks like in order to admire it, but we can also see what it should look like when it is broken and needs repair.

Before time or anything material existed, there was relationship. The triune God lived in perfect agreement from eternity past. Genesis 1:26 gives us a glimpse into how Father, Son, and Holy Spirit interacted with each other:

> Then God said, "Let us make man in our image, after our likeness. And let them have dominion over the fish of the sea and over the birds of the heavens and over the livestock and over all the earth and over every creeping thing that creeps on the earth."

Being in relationship and being part of a broken relationship have been a theme throughout all of humanity. Even though the triune God had never experienced brokenness in relationship, he knew at creation that he himself would have to live the pain that a fragmented relationship would bring. At that very moment in history, God the Father knew he would have to turn his back on the Son. The Son also understood that because of the act of creation, he would experience the incomprehensible pain of separation from the Father. The triune God, who had always experienced fullness of joy in relationship, subjected himself completely to entering into all of the sorrows of relationship.

We get another view into this happiness the Trinity experienced in relationship when Jesus was baptized by John:

> And when Jesus was baptized, immediately he went up from the water, and behold, the heavens were opened to him, and he saw the Spirit of God descending like a dove and coming to rest on him; and behold, a voice from heaven said, "This is my beloved Son, with whom I am well pleased."
>
> Matthew 3:16–17

The pleasure that the Trinity experiences in relationship is something that here on earth we will never understand—complete agreement, complete pleasure, complete unity. As Jesus was baptized he was identifying himself with sinners, and the Father proclaimed his pleasure. On the cross, when Jesus actually became the sin of the sinners, the Father turned his back. All this so that we could know relationship in a new way.

Matthew Henry puts it this way:

> The affection the Father had for him; He *is my beloved Son;* his dear Son, *the Son of his love* (Col. 1:13); he has lain in his bosom from all eternity (Jn. 1:18), had been *always his delight* (Prov. 8:30), but particularly as Mediator, and in undertaking the work of man's salvation, he was his *beloved Son.* He is *my Elect, in whom my soul delights.* See Isa. 42:1. Because he consented to the covenant of redemption, and delighted to do that *will of God, therefore the Father loved him.* Jn. 10:17; 3:35. *Behold,* then, *behold,* and wonder, *what manner of love the Father has bestowed on us,* that he should deliver up him that was the Son of his love, to suffer and die for those that were the generation of his wrath; nay, and that he *therefore* loved him, *because he laid down his life for the sheep!* Now know we that he loved us, *seeing he has not withheld his Son, his only Son, his Isaac whom he loved,* but *gave him to be a sacrifice for our sin.*[1]

Adam and Eve

Since the triune God made humans in his image, we were made to be relational beings. The very first relationships we see in the Bible are a testament to that truth. Starting with Adam's relationship to God, the first pronouncement that God places over Adam is that "it is not good" for him to be alone (Genesis 2:18). God goes on to create relationship for Adam by giving him the woman, Eve. This first marriage was a beautiful evidence of how relationship was meant to be. The way that Adam describes Eve is lovely:

"This at last is bone of my bone and flesh of my flesh" (Genesis 2:23). What he found in Eve could not be found in relationship with the animals, and the happiness he experienced was not to be found alone. The vulnerability and openness between Adam and Eve was how relationship was intended to be: They were "naked and were not ashamed" (v. 25). Their openness, vulnerability, and ability to love without hiding was all part of the original plan. Adam and Eve were made in the image of God.

How many of us could truly describe our relationships with our parents, or spouse, or children, or friends, or co-workers as something where we are completely open and vulnerable? I would venture to say that most, if not all of us, have never experienced a relationship where we were completely honest about who we are. Now in some cases that might actually be a good thing. Confessing to your child that you sometimes wish they'd never been born would not be a good thing and should never be said, even in the interest of being honest. But I would also say that most of our lives are characterized by hiding who we truly are and how we feel. Let's go back to the Garden of Eden to see what happened to the perfect relationship of Adam and Eve.

At some point, Adam and Eve were walking in the garden and happened upon the "tree of the knowledge of good and evil" (Genesis 2:17)—the one tree from which God had commanded them not to eat. Eve, after a conversation with the snake, decided it was in her best interests to take and eat of the tree, and she then gave the fruit to her husband, who was with her (Genesis 3:1–7). This decision severed their relationship with God. He had given them a command and they had disobeyed that command, making the claim that they did not need him but would rather do things their own way. Interestingly enough, once they broke relationship with God, they immediately broke relationship with each other as well. And perhaps they broke relationship with each

30

other when they sinned together, but that comes out in a visible way when God confronts them, as we see in Genesis chapter 3:

> And they heard the sound of the Lord God walking in the garden in the cool of the day, and the man and his wife hid themselves from the presence of the Lord God among the trees of the garden. But the Lord God called to the man and said to him, "Where are you?" And he said, "I heard the sound of you in the garden, and I was afraid, because I was naked, and I hid myself." He said, "Who told you that you were naked? Have you eaten of the tree of which I commanded you not to eat?" The man said, "The woman whom you gave to be with me, she gave me fruit of the tree, and I ate." Then the Lord God said to the woman, "What is this that you have done?" The woman said, "The serpent deceived me, and I ate."

vv. 8–13

Martyn Lloyd-Jones comments on this passage brilliantly:

> This initial act of rebellion produced fear in them; once they knew they had done something they should not have done, that caused them to look at each other with jealousy and envy. Then the children came, and they were envious and jealous and so on; sorrow came after sorrow. And it can all be traced back to the fact that men and women were really meant to live a life in communion with God.[2]

Their relationship with each other and with God was without fear. Once fear of judgment entered the picture, all sorts of other ugliness followed. Adam blamed God and Eve, Eve blamed the serpent, and relationship was broken.

Even in this most ugly and sorrowful moment we see God's plan of redemption at work. We have two very serious problems here: Relationship with God was broken, and relationship between Adam and Eve was broken. There is one solution to both problems: God promises a Rescuer is coming. In Genesis 3:15, we catch a glimpse of what God has in store for the brokenness: "He shall bruise your head, and you shall bruise his heel." Romans 16:20 puts it a different way: "The God of peace will soon crush Satan under your feet. The grace of our Lord Jesus Christ be with you." God's grace comes crashing into the darkness of deception and blame-shifting. Instead of only giving judgment for their sin, he gives hope of redemption.

This hope of redemption is the only hope we have in relationships. We can learn, memorize, and try to put into practice twenty-five steps to a better marriage, or ten ways to be a better friend, or how to be a super-parent, but the truth is we can't live up to those steps. We will fail repeatedly. We will hurt the very people we are trying to love, and they will hurt us. When we really feel that we are the one trying in the relationship because we have memorized our twenty-five steps and are implementing a good nineteen of them, we will be judgmental and angry toward the other person in the relationship because they aren't even trying. When we feel like a failure because we know we can't even begin to love the way we should, we will hide and avoid being in relationship for fear of failure. Either way, when we are doing well or doing badly, we are focused on ourselves. This inward focus will be the very thing that keeps us from the end goal of having a healthy, thriving, God-glorifying relationship.

We must be enraptured with Jesus. Who he is and how he has loved us must fill our gaze. Once we do this, we will find that we are able to love the way we have been loved. We will be able to exhibit the kindness, patience, and forgiveness that has been shown to us. We will be free to be vulnerable and able to love without using others. We won't need anything from those we are in relationship with because every longing to be loved and accepted has been completely fulfilled in Christ. When our hearts are at rest in God's sustaining communion with us, we can be free to serve and be in true communion with others.

When confronted with their sin, Adam and Eve did exactly what you and I do today. They looked for an excuse, a reason to claim that their sin wasn't their fault. This destroys relationship, as inevitably we end up blaming each other for the way we act. The freedom of the gospel says we don't have to blame anybody else; we can take full responsibility for our own sin because we have been completely forgiven. Can you imagine a relationship where you own your sin without blame-shifting or excuse-making? Owning our own mess will make us gracious toward everybody else who is a mess also. We won't place crazy expectations on others, because we will know that we can't even fulfill those expectations ourselves. We won't withhold forgiveness, because we will see how much we have been forgiven. "Into this cycle breaks the message of the gospel, the message that, on the cross, God has levied our embarrassing stories on the innocent, in our place, so that we stand known before God without fear of hiding."[3]

The Command to Love

The command to love is on every believer's life. Interestingly enough, Adam and Eve didn't have to be told to love each other. Adam was immediately taken with Eve. After the Fall, however, it all changed. Now we have to be *told* to love one another. Of the Ten Commandments, six of them are instructions on how to love one another. (See Exodus 20:2–17.) Prohibitions on our now normal selfish bent would have been foreign to Adam and Eve. God had to define and set boundaries on what relationship should look like. Children need to honor their parents. We shouldn't take another person's life. We must stay committed to one spouse and not commit adultery. We shouldn't take the belongings of another person. We shouldn't lie about anybody. We shouldn't covet or desire anything of our neighbor's. Not only do these commands deal with outward actions—stealing, murder, adultery—they also deal with the heart, as in the command not to covet (v. 17).

If I am honest as I read these laws, I start to think that I can fulfill them. I feel a safety in my ability not to kill, commit adultery, steal. But then when we get to the part about not lying about anybody, and not coveting another person's things, I start to feel a little uncomfortable. I know for a fact that I have lied and coveted this very day. While driving my kids to school I saw a woman in a 1957 Chevy 3100 series pickup truck, painted—of course—cherry red. I have wanted that truck for as long as I can remember. I felt a little sad as I looked at it. I wondered why I didn't get to have a truck like that. The lie I believed in that moment was that an automobile would make me happy, would somehow bring meaning to my life. And although it is the greatest truck ever crafted in the history of the world, it won't bring lasting happiness.

In Leviticus 19:18 God commands us to love one another: "You shall not take vengeance or bear a grudge against the sons of your own people, but you shall love your neighbor as yourself: I am the Lord." We are also commanded to love God in Deuteronomy 6:4–5: "Hear, O Israel: The Lord our God, the Lord is one. You shall love the Lord your God with all your heart and with all your soul and with all your might."

Jesus reinforces the command to love in Matthew 22:37–40:

> You shall love the Lord your God with all your heart and with all your soul and with all your mind. This is the great and first

commandment. And a second is like it: You shall love your neighbor as yourself. On these two commandments depend all the Law and the Prophets.

Christ tells us that the entire law is summed up in loving God and loving others. Again in John 15:12, Jesus says, "This is my commandment, that you love one another as I have loved you." With this verse we are not only commanded to love, but to love as Christ has loved us.

Now, I know I am not anywhere near having that type of love for anybody. Even on my best days, when I feel loving and want to be kind, my actions are still laced with selfishness. Let me explain. There are times when I do loving acts for my family because I feel guilty. I try to make an extra nice meal for them because I haven't been the kindest person. There are also times when I do loving acts for those around me because I want something in return. If I help you move, that means you will help *me* move when the time comes.

There are also times when I am extra kind because I want to shame others for the way they have treated me. For example, I had a friend who had promised to be praying for me as I was speaking at a conference. She also told me she would text me and let me know when she prayed. After speaking all day, I had received no text and was fairly certain that no prayers had been offered on my behalf. I was angry and felt neglected. Instead of showing my anger by ignoring her or by sending an angry text, I sent a very sweet, well-crafted text telling my friend I had been thinking about her and praying for her. My hope in sending this text was not to love on her or to have her feel blessed but rather to show her how real friends act. I am ashamed to admit that was the intent of my heart, but it absolutely was. There are times when I do loving acts so that people think well of me. Often my loving acts end up being merely for myself.

Charles Spurgeon tells a story that illustrates this type of "love" perfectly.

Once upon a time there was a king who ruled over everything in a land. One day there was a gardener who grew an enormous carrot. He took it to his king and said, "My Lord, this is the greatest carrot I've ever grown or ever will grow; therefore, I want to present it to you as a token of my love and respect for you." The king was touched and discerned the man's heart, so as he turned to go, the king said, "Wait! You are clearly a good steward of the earth. I want to give a plot of land to you freely as a gift, so you can garden it all." The gardener was amazed and delighted and went home rejoicing. But there was a nobleman at the king's court who overheard all this, and he said, "My! If that is what you get for a carrot, what if you gave the king something better?" The next day the nobleman came before the king, and he was leading a handsome black stallion. He bowed low and said, "My Lord, I breed horses, and this is the greatest horse I've ever bred or ever will; therefore, I want to present it to you as a token of my love and respect for you." But the king discerned his heart and said, "Thank you," and took the horse and simply dismissed him. The nobleman was perplexed, so the king said, "Let me explain. That gardener was giving me the carrot, but you were giving yourself the horse."[4]

Often in my relationships, I am giving myself the horse through acts of kindness to others.

In Matthew 5, Jesus puts the nail in the coffin of our self-reliance. He takes those Ten Commandments that talk about outward obedience and pushes them to apply to our hearts. When at one time I might have felt okay when I read "Don't commit adultery," now I am undone when I learn that if I look at anyone with "lustful intent" I am guilty of breaking that command (v. 28). And I know

I haven't murdered anybody, so I feel righteous about my ability to keep that command, but now I read that if I am angry with my brother, I am "liable to judgment" (v. 22). I have broken that command most days by the time my kids are off to school. With the truth before me that I don't love the way I am commanded to love, I start to see my need for a Savior. I see my need for a rescuer.

Jesus takes these commands even a step further in John 13:34–35: "A new commandment I give to you, that you love one another: just as I have loved you, you also are to love one another. By this all people will know that you are my disciples, if you have love for one another." The way people will know that we are Christians is by our love for one another. Yet again, he asks us to love others the way he has loved us. He gives this "new command" right after he washes the feet of Judas. He knowingly washes the feet of the one who is set to betray him. This call to love others this way seems impossible. I can barely be kind to the person that cuts me off on the freeway. Love my enemies? Do good to those who hate me? Serve those that I know are set to kill me? Sometimes I get angry because I have to make dinner for my family, and I actually do love them more than anybody on the earth. I fall so incredibly short of obeying the command to love, not only in my heart but also in my actions.

More than that, 1 John 2:9 tells us that if we claim to be Christians and hate our brothers, we are still in darkness. If the overarching theme of your life is hate for others, you are not a Christian. The command to love is high and lofty. The importance of loving others is not negotiable.

The Point of the Law

It is not just good advice to love the way that Jesus loves. It is a command from a holy God to sinful people. This holy God cannot dismiss my sin and think, *Well, she tried a little bit. That's going to count.* The Bible tells us that the "wages of sin is death" (Romans 6:23). God does not wink at sin. He takes our sin very seriously, to the point of demanding that blood be shed to pay for our sin. We often pick up a book on relationships and think, *If I can just learn how to love people better, I will be a better person, a better Christian.* God demands complete perfection, a complete fulfilling of the Law. He doesn't ask us to love the best we can. He demands that we love with everything we are all the time. We cannot do that. So what is the point?

Martin Luther gives us three reasons for the Law:

> First, the Law helps to control violent outbursts of sin and to keep order in the world (curb). Second, the Law accuses us and shows us our sin (mirror). Third, the Law teaches us Christians what we should and should not do to live a God-pleasing life (a guide). The power to live according to the Law comes from the Gospel.[5]

Applying this specifically to the area of relationships and loving people, first we are told to love others the way Jesus has loved us in order to control us. If I know that it is against the law of the land and against the law of God to kill someone, I will think twice about doing it. Second, when looking at the way I love others, I see a severe discrepancy in the way I am commanded to love and the way I actually love. The law to love shows me that I am a sinner and I need a Savior. Third, when I see that I am commanded to love, I know what I need to do in order to live a life of grateful obedience for what he has done for me.

"Love as I have loved you" is not just a nice saying that Christians should have on a print hanging in their homes. It is meant to crush you. It is meant to show you how in and of yourself you cannot love the way that Christ has loved you. I could fill the pages of this book with all the commands from God to you about how to love. I could expound on those laws and add personal experiences and general guidelines on how to fulfill those laws. I could also wax eloquent on the times that I or others have loved sacrificially and hope that inspires you. Instead, I hope that you have heard the word of the Law—"love perfectly"—and have seen how you don't do that and how desperately you need help. My guess is that if you have picked up a book on relationships, you are fully aware that you don't have it all together. That's a good place to start. My hope is that we never get past that. It is in that place of humility that God meets us and pours his grace out on us.

May we never get to the place where we feel like we know how to do relationships perfectly, because once we get there we will no longer feel our need for the Holy Spirit. As I said in the introduction, the point of this book is not to give you a push in the right direction. We need more than a push. We need to be made alive. We are not basically good people who need a little instruction so that we can live up to our full potential. We are completely sinful people who need help from outside of ourselves in order to be made alive.

The purpose of the law is to crush, but God doesn't leave us there. Praise him for his glorious grace! He never leaves us crushed. In all of the verses that I have shared with you in this chapter, there have been glimpses of the gospel. There have been hints toward healing. In the next chapter we will talk about how we can begin to love as we have been loved. First take some time to reflect and repent. Repentance is a good thing as long as you remember that every way you have failed to love has been paid for by Jesus Christ. He took those wages of sin upon himself. He paid the penalty for our sin. He paid for every self-ish act, every unloving glance, every angry moment, when he died on the cross for our sins. We are covered completely with his righteousness. In all the ways we have failed in relationships, he lived and loved perfectly. We can be grateful for his perfect obedience because that record is now ours. We are dressed in his righteousness alone. It is good to be very aware that you fail as long as you remember that he didn't and that he loves us regardless of our failures.

3

How Do We Change?

As I mentioned in the introduction, there are countless books on Amazon about relationships—many from a Christian perspective—and yet our relationships don't seem to be getting better. I believe the problem is that we are going at relationships from the wrong direction. We are looking at what we can do to better ourselves with the hopes that it will better those around us too, and we are throwing in a couple Bible verses about what love should look like to back up our point. I believe our focus needs to be on our *primary* relationship, instead of our secondary relationships. If all we needed was a little relationship advice, then why would Jesus Christ have to come and die for our sins in order to bring us into relationship?

The world tells you that if you love well, you will be loved. Christ's very life is evidence against the validity of that statement. Was there ever a man who loved so purely, loved men without the need to compete, loved women without the need to use, loved his parents without the need to throw off restraint, loved strangers even when he was exhausted, loved his enemies without seeking revenge? Truly he loved his own unto the very end. And yet, he was betrayed, forsaken, denied, and mercilessly crucified for his life of selfless service. Jesus went so far as to say, "Woe to you, when all people speak well of you" (Luke 6:26). Truly our suffering Savior understood the pain of relationships. "He came to his own, and his own people did not receive him" (John 1:11). I get angry when I do something small for my husband and he doesn't respond with gratitude. Imagine the pain Christ felt when every second of his day was an offering of love and that offering was taken and trampled.

Too High/Too Low

We have too high a view of our ability to do things right if we just have the right instructions. And for the most part we can sort of keep it together . . . at least outwardly, or at least we think we can. I can say all the right "Christian" things and try to smile when someone has upset me, but inside I am seething.

For instance, just last night I got home from a busy day and my husband had gotten home a little before me. He was watching TV and had had a terrible day. I, of course, wanted to be the one who deserved to be tired from having a hard day, so when I saw his demeanor I knew he wasn't up for my belly-aching. I tried to be nice, offering to fix a quick dinner and asking him about his day, but my heart was a tornado. I was angry that he wasn't asking about *my* day. I was mad that I was always the one who had to cook dinner even though I had worked that day too, and on and on. Again, get the picture? Outwardly I was smiling and trying to serve, but inwardly I was angry. Add to this that I had a self-righteous heart in thinking I was the one who was serving when I didn't feel like it, while he got to just be down. I was pretty sure I had pulled off the charade, too, until I sat down next to him and he said, "You don't seem okay. Is something wrong?"

Here I was thinking the whole time I was fulfilling my duty in relationship, and the honest truth was, he was the one who was actually concerned about me. I was concerned about doing it right. We can get so caught up in the doing that we forget about the people we are supposed to love. Here is another reason I think most relationship books are off: They focus on the doing.

Though you and I would probably never verbalize this, I believe we also have too low a view of God and his love for us. In our laser-like attention to the doing, we forget what has been done. We forget how God has loved us with an everlasting love, and that his steadfast love will endure forever. And in the times that we actually remember, we don't think it is enough. We have heard that his love should be supreme, but we don't feel it and we don't know it.

Let me illustrate. I can tell you that I am holding the most delicious piece of dark chocolate. I can show you the wrapper and you can see that it reads *Godiva Dark Chocolate* on the label. You can look at the bar and see that it looks like dark chocolate. Or I can give you a piece of it (but not the whole thing because I am selfish), and you can take that piece of chocolate and put it in your mouth and feel the smoothness of it as it melts, while the bitter sweetness of it embraces your taste buds, and the smell overwhelms your senses, and at that moment you can know: This is dark chocolate. In that instant, it will become your treasure.

My hope is that this book will help you "taste and see that the Lord is good" (Psalm 34:8). That as I open up to you all that he is and all that he has done, your senses will be overwhelmed and he will be your treasure. As you taste this multifaceted relationship with God, it will transform all of your other relationships. Not just because you want to be a better person, but also because you will be so astounded by all the ways he chooses to relate to you and *how* he chooses to relate to you that you won't be able to help being changed.

Do/Done

As I wrote previously, you won't find a lot of advice in this book. That's because I want to dwell on the tasting. I want you to be so enthralled with God's love for you in Christ that you will run around loving people with everything that you are. While most books on relationships will focus on the *do*—what you should do, when you should do it, how you should do it—I want to focus on the *done*. How has God been your Father? How has Jesus tied himself to you as your brother? What does it mean that Jesus has made you his friend? Focusing on what he has *already* done for you will fill you with such a freedom and liberty that you will find relationships easier. I am not saying relationships will be easy, but as your focus changes they will become easier because they will have less to do with others and yourself and more to do with the one constant in your life, the truth that "his steadfast love endures forever" (Psalm 107:1).To be real honest, the *doing* will work out differently in each relationship. What is good for my husband may not be good for yours. What is helpful to my kids may not be helpful to yours. This creates a new dynamic where you have to know and invest in people. There is no "one size fits all" when it comes to relationships.

The whole Bible is written in such a way that in most verses we see the *done* before we see the *do*. But, unfortunately, you and I are blind to it. We love thinking about ourselves, and since the *do* is about us, we prefer to think about that. And you and I think so highly of ourselves and our abilities, we are certain we can actually do the *do*.

Let me give you an example of how we can find the *do* and *done* in most passages of Scripture. First John 4:11 says, "Beloved, if God so loved us, we also ought to love one another." Most of us would read that verse and think rightly that *I should love others*. This is our take-away from that verse. But we've skipped right over the beginning. The very first word of that verse should cause us to worship in joyful adoration. "Beloved" means "one who is in a very special relationship with another, *only, only beloved*."[1] So many people search their entire lives to have someone call them their "beloved" or their "one and only." We want a special or unique relationship where we are assured of affection and welcome. But the very thing we are looking for, we already have. It is already done. The verse doesn't say, "God is looking for you to get your act together so that he can love you." Instead, the verse starts out with a declaration over you and over me. You are named; you are loved; you are in relationship. Soak that in for a minute. Before you move on, think on this: God calls you his beloved.

The verse goes on to say, "if God so loved us." How exactly did he love us? Let's look back to the verse preceding this one in order to see. "In this is love, not that we have loved God but that he loved us and sent his Son to be the propitiation for our sins" (v. 10). So, before we ever had a thought of loving God, his love was pursuing us. He was loving without being loved in return. It wasn't a distant, inactive love. It was an intimate, life-giving love. He loved us by giving us the most costly thing to him. He gave us his Son.

This gift changes everything for us. It isn't a gift that is just a "nice thought" but is in actuality useless to you. He gave Jesus to become a propitiation for our sins. That word *propitiation* means to turn away wrath. God so desired relationship with us, he wanted to love us deeply, but he couldn't because he is holy and cannot bear to be around sin. His holiness makes him rightly angry at sin, so in turn he would always be angry with us because we are always sinning. So what does he do with his anger toward us? He pours it out on himself; he pours it out on the Son. I have heard it said that only God himself could bear the full wrath for all of our sins. That he did. He bore the wrath.

He didn't do it for people who were in love with him either. He gave the Son, and the Son gave his life *before* we loved him. We were, in fact, his enemies and hated him. We were unworthy of his love, and yet his heart beat with compassion for us. This is what has been *done*. He bore the weight of the wrath of God. He loved us before we loved him. Now, think about that as we hear the *do*—so now "love each other." It seems so small in comparison to what he has done. For there is nobody who has sinned against me like I have sinned against him.

The *Do* Is Good

"Blessed is the man who walks not in the counsel of the wicked, nor stands in the way of sinners, nor sits in the seat of scoffers; but *his delight is in the law of the Lord*, and on his law he meditates day and night" (Psalm 1:1–2, emphasis mine). The *law of the Lord*, or the *do* that I have been talking about, is a good thing. When we shift our focus from the *do* to the *done*, it's easy to then think that the *do* isn't important or worth pursuing. But the rules that God has laid out for us are beautiful. His wisdom is inscrutable and his love is never-ending. Like a good father, he knows what is best for us and gives us good instruction in his Word. All of the commands of Scripture are perfect and right.

There is one problem with the commands, though—they don't have the power to change us. They may have the power to change our outward actions, but when it comes to the heart, only the Holy Spirit has the power to take a heart of stone and turn it into a heart of flesh. We could have all the knowledge in the world on how to be a loving person, but if we don't have the Holy Spirit working in and through us, we will never truly change. Even if you were a relationship guru, and loved the way you knew you should love, you would still need to do more to be accepted by God. Romans 10:4 says, "For Christ is the end of the law for righteousness to everyone who believes." You and I need more than the "how to be a better wife" talk. We need a Savior. We need someone to come and fulfill all the *do's* perfectly on our behalf so that we can stand before a holy God who judges not only our actions but also our thoughts and intentions, and have him accept us. Christ put an end to being accepted on the basis of our always doing the right thing. He did it for us. So while the *do* is good and important to look at, it isn't enough.

We don't just need a new list; we need a new heart. That is exactly what is promised to us in Ezekiel 11:19–20:

> And I will give them one heart, and a new spirit I will put within them. I will remove the heart of stone from their flesh and give them a heart of flesh, that they may walk in my statutes and keep my rules and obey them. And they shall be my people, and I will be their God.

The only way you and I will ever be able to obey is if our hearts are moved and changed by the work of the Holy Spirit. The Israelites knew God's law better than anybody and yet they needed a new heart in order to be able to obey. Obedience is more than following the rules; obedience must come from a heart of love, or it is nothing more than self-righteousness.

Becoming Enraptured

In order to have this heart of gratefulness, we must have something to be grateful for. That happens when the Holy Spirit enlivens our hearts to the beauty of his love. We change when our affections change. Thomas Chalmers, in his landmark sermon "The Expulsive Power of a New Affection," says this:

> It is when released from the spirit of bondage with which love cannot dwell, and when admitted into the number of God's children through the faith that is in Christ Jesus, the spirit of adoption is poured upon us—it is then that the heart, brought under the mastery of one great and predominant affection, is delivered from the tyranny of its former desires, in the only way in which deliverance is possible.[2]

We can't just tell ourselves to be better friends and then, *shazam!* we are. We must be captivated by the way that Jesus has befriended us and how he has met all of our needs for companionship. Once this is clear to us and we take hold of it, we will then be able to be the friend we need to be.

Our affections need to be fixed on, found in, rooted and grounded in the love of Christ. Paul prays this very thing for the people of Ephesus:

> For this reason I bow my knees before the Father, from whom every family in heaven and on earth is named, that according to the riches of his glory he may grant you to be strengthened with power through his Spirit in your inner being, so that Christ may dwell in your hearts through faith—that you, being rooted and

grounded in love, may have strength to comprehend with all the saints what is the breadth and length and height and depth, and to know the love of Christ that surpasses knowledge, that you may be filled with all the fullness of God. Now to him who is able to do far more abundantly than all that we ask or think, according to the power at work within us, to him be glory in the church and in Christ Jesus throughout all generations, forever and ever. Amen.

Ephesians 3:14–21

Paul doesn't pray that the Ephesians would get their act together; he prays that they would somehow be able to comprehend the incomprehensible love of God in Christ. This is my prayer for you as you read this book. This is my prayer for my children, this is my prayer for my husband, and this is my prayer for myself—that we would understand this love and see this love in everything, and as we see this love learn to love each other. This love fills us with the fullness of God. This has been done—the fixing of his love for us in eternity past—and it is far more beautiful than the *do*. The Holy Spirit is the one at work within us, reminding us of this truth. And as he reminds us, we are changed. You and I fall less in love with the world, we care less about what the world thinks of us, we find less of our identity in how our spouse and others treat us, and we see the height, the depth, the length of God's love for us in Christ.

4

God Our Father and Our Relationships With Our Children

Putting Aside Our Past

*T*he glorious truth that God calls himself our Father can be complicated for many people. The word *father* may have all sorts of baggage for you. You may have hated your father, or been abused or ignored by him, or possibly never even known him. Your father may have been an angry man, unforgiving, or merciless. Your father may have been depressed, quiet, and detached. Or possibly you have had the kindest, godliest father in the world. My prayer is that all of your ideas of what a father should or shouldn't be would be suspended for a while as you read this chapter. Maybe you could even take a moment and pray that the Holy Spirit would give you amnesia about your childhood, or even your adult relationship with your father, and that you would hear what the Bible tells us about God being our Father. I even ask that if *you* are a father, you would not compare yourself to what you are going to read here. Let's just take this time to sit and learn about our heavenly Father without any thought of ourselves or our past. As we do this, I pray that a healing will take place in your heart if you are wounded, that the joy of being loved by your heavenly Father would eclipse all other thoughts.

Why Us?

God has chosen by his good pleasure to make us his children. Jeremiah 31:9 puts it this way: "With weeping they shall come, and with pleas for mercy I will lead them back, I will make them walk by brooks of water, in a straight path in which they shall not stumble, *for I am a father to Israel, and Ephraim is my firstborn*" (emphasis mine). God took the name of *Father* upon himself. He chose to make the relationship familial. We are "by nature children of wrath" (Ephesians 2:3), but God in his mercy set his love upon us. This love has changed us. It has changed our very nature. His love has changed who we belong to. Those on whom God has set his love are no longer children of wrath, but have been brought into God's family and are now referred to as "children of God" (1 John 3:1).

The question is why. Why has God chosen to relate to us as our Father? Why has God adopted us into his family? The answer is found in Ephesians 1:4–6:

> He chose us in him before the foundation of the world, that we should be holy and blameless before him. In love he predestined us for adoption as sons through Jesus Christ, according to the purpose of his will, to the praise of his glorious grace, with which he has blessed us in the Beloved.

The answer is his love. According to this verse, he chose us before we were born. Before we had done anything right or wrong, he decided we would be a part of his family. This adoption into his family came to him at a great cost. He had to go about making his enemies his family. As we talked about earlier, God cannot just wink at sin, or turn a blind eye. Our sins had to be done away with in order for us to have a relationship with him. He does this "through Jesus Christ" (v. 5). Because of Christ, our brother, we are now welcomed into the family of God.

It's Legal

We have a dear family friend whose name is Summer. My children adore her. Well, the truth is, we all do. Summer isn't related to our family in any way, although she feels like a part of us. My children decided to start calling her Auntie Summie. This term of endearment shows their love for her and that, as far as they are concerned, she is their aunt. This is a very sweet sentiment, and I love that they love her that much, but she is not legally a part of our family. If there is an inheritance that all of my siblings and I share, Summer will not get any part of it.

But our relationship with God is different. He doesn't just call us his children. The use of the word *adoption* in these verses is a legal term. We are legally and irrevocably part of his forever family. God has said to us, "All that is mine is yours. You are my children. I won't hold anything good back from you."

Our Part

What do we have to do in order to become a part of his family? John 1:12–13 gives us our role. "But to all who did receive him, who believed in his name, he gave the right to become children of God, who were born, not of blood nor of the will of the flesh nor of the will of man, but of God." We are called to believe. Sounds too easy, right? Seems like we should have to prove ourselves, to somehow show that we are serious about being his children. John tells us that it's not because of our will, not because of anything we have done or will do, but because God has decided to accept us. We have been born again. We are no longer who we once were, but we are now children of the living God. How great must his love for us be that he would make us his own without any deserving on our part.

Adoption

J. I. Packer says that this adoption into the family of God is the highest and best privilege of being a believer. He talks about how justification—having our sins forgiven and being made right in God's eyes—is a very good thing, but his stance is that adoption is even greater.

> Adoption is higher, because of the richer relationship with God that it involves. . . . Justification is a *forensic* idea, conceived in terms of *law*, and viewing God as *judge*. . . . Adoption is a *family* idea, conceived in terms of *love*, and viewing God as *father*. In adoption, God takes us into His family and fellowship, and establishes us as His children and heirs. Closeness, affection and generosity are at the heart of the relationship. To be right with God the judge is a great thing, *but to be loved and cared for by God the father is a greater.*[1]

He also goes on to say, "Our understanding of Christianity cannot be better than our grasp on adoption."[2]

Brothers and sisters, we must see and relish the importance of God being our Father. This will inform how we relate to him.

He has related to us out of love, kindness, and tenderness. We can in turn relate to him without any fear.

Our Good Father

Relating to God as our Father is a matter of trust. Do we really trust that he is as good as he claims to be? He calls to us to believe in his goodness. He wants us to trust in his mercy extended to us. By nature we are suspicious of anybody who does good to us without our deserving it. We are enslaved to our popular notion of karma: If we are good little boys and girls, God will be a good Father. We live by the rule "If it seems too good to be true, it probably is." If someone gives us an expensive gift, we are always wondering what they want in return. It is almost painful for us to receive without earning. When we go out to dinner with a friend and they offer to pay the bill, we always offer to get the tip. We have to somehow make it even. We can't be in someone's debt. It strips us of our self-reliance, makes us feel "less-than." In actuality, that is a really good place to be. We are also wary of God when we disobey. We believe that if we are bad, he is just waiting to unleash his wrath on us. The truth is that he has already unleashed his wrath on his Son for all of our badness.

I have a dear friend who is rehabbing a house for her parents, who just moved to be close to her and her family. She and her husband have spent countless hours organizing laborers and doing work themselves in order to make this house livable and nice for her parents. We were talking about the process the other day and she was telling me how hard it is for her parents to accept their gift of doing all the work for free. This is so true for all of us. If anybody should be able to accept a gift, it is your parents, who have served and given to you your whole life. But still, it is our nature not to like taking without paying back. It is humbling to accept a gift of great magnitude. In essence, it is to admit we are needy, and our hearts hate that.

God is a good father who loves blessing his children. In Matthew 7:9–11, Jesus gives us an example of how to relate to a father who loves to bless his children:

> Which one of you, if his son asks him for bread, will give him a stone? Or if he asks for a fish, will give him a serpent? If you then, who are evil, know how to give good gifts to your children, how much more will your Father who is in heaven give good things to those who ask him!

Get a picture in your mind of the kindest father you have ever known. This verse is calling that father evil compared to how God fathers you. He is not the type of father who is happy with you one day and angry the next. He doesn't have a bad day at work and then come home and take it out on you. He is a good father who gives good gifts, always.

See!

"See what kind of love the Father has given to us, that we should be called children of God; and so we are" (1 John 3:1). The point of seeing God as our Father is to revel in his love. His love is a gift that was given to us. It was a costly gift. His love caused him to give his Son. John 3:16 is one of the most used and least understood verses of the Bible. We reduce that verse to a "get saved quick" pill instead of plumbing its depths for the richness of the love displayed. God loved and he gave. He initiated this act of drawing us into his family. Again, all he is calling you to do is believe. Believe that he loves you; believe that he wants you in his family.

There are no black sheep in this family. We have all been washed white in the blood of the Lamb. He doesn't love one child more than another. He loves each of us as he loves Jesus. In his High Priestly Prayer, Jesus asks God "that the world may know that you sent me and loved them even as you loved me" (John 17:23). How does God love Christ? Think about that for just a moment. Don't rush past this. God loves Christ without any hint of displeasure. God loves Christ joyfully. God loves Christ completely. God loves Christ with such a fullness and unity we cannot even begin to comprehend it. This, Beloved, is also how God loves us. There is complete welcome awaiting us.

Jesus prayed this right before he went to his death. He knew that bringing us eternally into the family of God would cost him everything. See! This is the love that the triune God has for us, a love that is willing to give everything. His love withholds no good thing. We can trust him; we can trust this love. We don't have to be afraid.

No Slavery/No Fear

> For all who are led by the Spirit of God are sons of God. For you did not receive the spirit of slavery to fall back into fear, but you have received the Spirit of adoption as sons, by whom we cry, "Abba! Father!" The Spirit himself bears witness with our spirit that we are children of God.
>
> Romans 8:14–16

Here is yet another benefit of knowing and being secure in our relationship with our Father. We don't have to be afraid. We don't have to shrink back from God. So many of us live in this state of fear, wondering if God will love us today. Part of the Holy Spirit's work in our lives is to convince us that we are actually children of God. It is such an unbelievable privilege that we need the work of a miracle to show us it is true. God doesn't desire a relationship that is based on fear. God desires a relationship based on intimacy.

Our pastor lives on the same street as a Jewish family. The father of the family is a Hasidic priest, and he has two very sweet daughters. They follow all the ceremonial laws of the Old Testament. One Wednesday evening we were over at our pastor's house. The little girls were outside playing with my kids and my pastor's children. I looked down the street and saw the father walking toward the group of children. One of his daughters saw him walking toward us and started yelling, "Abba! Abba!" She then took off in a sprint running down the street toward her dad. The smile on his face was visible from half a block away. She finally reached him and jumped into his arms. He laughed and held her.

This is a picture of what our relationship with God is like. He is our Abba Father, our Daddy. He is not some stern, distant judge that is perpetually disappointed with us. He is walking toward us, waiting for us to run and jump into his arms. The Holy Spirit's job is to persuade us that this is actually okay. Even as I write this I feel a little disrespectful, like maybe I have crossed a line, but these are his words. This is his truth. God was the one who inspired Paul to write these words in Romans.

Our hearts see the holiness of God and we want to cry out with Paul in Romans 7:24: "Wretched man that I am!" And the Spirit's work is to convince us that our next words uttered can be "Abba! Father!"

In all of our feelings of inadequacy, in all of our distrust of God's love, he calls to us over and over, repeating this phrase from Hosea 1: "And in the place where it was said to them, 'You are not my people,' it shall be said to them, 'Children of the living God.'" (v. 10). We were once not a people. We were once alienated. We were once orphans. But now, because of the blood of Christ, we have been brought near. We are now "children of the living God."

Fatherly Care

God describes his fatherly care for us in several different ways. Isaiah 1:2 talks about how God "reared and brought up" his children. That word *reared* can also be translated *nourished*. See what tenderness he uses with us. This same idea is seen in Hosea 11:1–4:

> When Israel was a child, I loved him, and out of Egypt I called my son. The more they were called, the more they went away; they kept sacrificing to the Baals and burning offerings to idols. Yet it was I who taught Ephraim to walk; I took them up by their arms, but they did not know that I healed them. I led them with cords of kindness, with the bands of love, and I became to them as one who eases the yoke on their jaws, and I bent down to them and fed them.

This description couldn't be more representative of the Christian walk. We are loved, we are called sons, and yet we continue to walk away. We continue to choose idols. We continue to look for the very love and the very joy that is already ours. And yet, his love for us doesn't stop. He teaches us and heals us, even though we don't give him credit. God's fatherly love looks like being led "with cords of kindness" and " bands of love." It looks like his bending down and feeding us. Understand that this love is not because Israel or we deserve it or have earned it. This condescension is right in the middle of our chasing idols. This is how great and how strong his love is for his children.

His tenderness toward us is shown by how he fights for us and carries us:

> The Lord your God who goes before you will himself fight for you, just as he did for you in Egypt before your eyes, and in the wilderness, where you have seen how the Lord your God carried you, as a man carries his son, all the way that you went until you came to this place.
>
> Deuteronomy 1:30–31

Again, in Isaiah, we see this picture of a God who carries his children:

> For he said, "Surely they are my people, children who will not deal falsely." And he became their Savior. In all their affliction he was afflicted, and the angel of his presence saved them; in his love and in his pity he redeemed them; *he lifted them up and carried them all the days of old.*
>
> 63:8–9, emphasis mine

Do you doubt his compassion for you? In all of your afflictions he is afflicted. He feels what you feel.

Listen to the tender heartbeat of our God for his children:

> But the Lord's portion is his people, Jacob his allotted heritage. He found him in a desert land, and in the howling waste of the wilderness; he encircled him, he cared for him, he kept him as the apple of his eye. Like an eagle that stirs up its nest, that flutters over its young, spreading out its wings, catching them, bearing them on its pinions, the Lord alone guided him.
>
> Deuteronomy 32:9–12

How can we read these words of endearment and doubt his fatherly concern for every aspect of our lives? He has kept you and me as the apple of his eye. Could there be a warmer love than the love that God has for his children? His fatherly concern guides us through every season of our lives. God even describes his care for us as a mother who cares for her children: "As one whom his mother comforts, so I will comfort you" (Isaiah 66:13).

I find it so interesting that the primary way Jesus tells us to address God is as "our Father in heaven" (Matthew 6:9). No longer do we address him as judge or as God Most High. He is all of those things, but to us he is our Father. This wasn't how the Jews would typically address God in prayer; this was a revolutionary thought. Not only does Jesus tell them to address God as Father, but also includes *our*. This speaks to us of community. It says that we are a family and that even our relationship with God is in the community of a family. The word *heaven* reminds us that even though he is close like a father, he is also otherworldly and transcendent. Tying "our Father in heaven" together displays a new way of relating to God.

God's Discipline

Society today equates discipline with anger. Discipline is connected to negative emotion. This could partially be because we discipline out of anger ourselves, or we have been disciplined by someone who was angry. The biblical definition of discipline, however, has no negative connotations at all. As a matter of fact, whenever God talks about disciplining his children, it is always in the context of love and delight. This is a total paradigm shift for us. We connect correction with disappointment, but God's correction of us has absolutely nothing to do with his being disappointed with us. Proverbs 3:11–12 says, "My son, do not despise the Lord's discipline or be weary of his reproof, for the

Lord reproves him whom he loves, as a father the son in whom he delights." Also, according to Hebrews 12, God's discipline of us is proof that we are his children.

Now, don't get me wrong. Discipline isn't some leisurely walk around a beautiful lake with the wind blowing slightly and the birds singing their melodies. Discipline is painful for us. Hebrews 12 confirms this by saying, "For the moment all discipline seems painful rather than pleasant, but later it yields the peaceful fruit of righteousness to those who have been trained by it" (v. 11). The point of God's discipline of us is to instill peace and righteousness, not to show us how angry he is at us. We confuse God's wrath for his enemies and his discipline of his children, but the two have nothing in common. God has no wrath left for his children. He has only love and pleasure and delight. This makes no sense to us. In our karma religion we reduce God's love to a capricious, flighty emotion that changes depending on how we are doing. This is not the love we have been learning about. This is not the love that says, "From everlasting to everlasting I have loved you." God does discipline us, but it is a fatherly concern that takes its little child and says, "This is the way, walk in it" (Isaiah 30:21).

When we are disobeying God and looking to idols and other loves to satisfy us, all the while God is grieving for us. He knows that there are pleasures forevermore at his right hand. His stance toward us is as a father who looks at his child who is missing out on something unbelievably beautiful to chase down something destructive. He gives us difficult circumstances to draw our hearts back to him. It is interesting to me that right after the verses on discipline in Hebrews 12, there is this: "Therefore lift your drooping hands and strengthen your weak knees, and make straight paths for your feet, so that what is lame may not be put out of joint but rather be healed" (vv. 12–13). God isn't trying to beat us down with his discipline. His goal is to strengthen us and make life easier for us. He isn't standing in heaven looking down his nose at us, saying, "Well, that is what you get for being so naughty."

He did look down from heaven at one point and his full wrath was poured out on his only Son for all that we have done. If you are wondering what God's wrath toward sin looks like, all you need to do is look at the bloody cross. His turning his face away from Christ is what wrath looks like. His forsaking of his Son was brought about by anger at our sin. And yet, we don't ever have to worry about his position toward us. He poured out the full cup of his wrath on Jesus. There is nothing left. He isn't an angry father looking to wield his power and authority to show us who is boss. Jesus felt the fullness of God's hatred for sin so that we could feel the fullness of God's love for righteousness: "Now may our Lord Jesus Christ himself, and God our Father, who loved us and gave us eternal comfort and good hope through grace, comfort your hearts and establish them in every good work and word" (2 Thessalonians 2:16–17).

What Does This Have to Do With My Kids?

We have seen what our heavenly Father is like, and how he has loved you as his child. So how does this change your relationship with your children? The answer to that question is, in every way possible. How the Father has loved you and cared for you and tenderly guided you has everything to do with how you treat your children. Take another look at the verse from 2 Thessalonians in the previous section. God himself has taught us how to love. The truth that God is your faithful Father gently carrying you through the hardships of parenting will change how you parent. The more you soak your heart in the truth that he has loved you despite yourself, the more you will be able to love the way you have been loved.

Our identity must come from being a child of God, not from being the parent of little Danny. We often look for our identity in how our children act. When they are sweet boys and girls, we feel like we are good parents. We erroneously think we did it right and that is why they turned out so good. We become prideful, arrogant, and merciless with parents whose children are not "good" like ours. We go around dispensing parenting advice as if we are the experts. We sound eerily similar to the Pharisee in Jesus' parable of the tax collector and the Pharisee. We may not exactly say, "Thank God I am not like them" (see Luke 18:11). But we do say or think things like, "I don't agree with their parenting style. Just look at how awful their kids are." The problem with this is, of course, that it leaves the Holy Spirit and how he works completely out of the equation. We think that if we are good parents, we will have good children. This is not the case. In the book *Give Them Grace,* my mom (Elyse Fitzpatrick) and I talk about this very idea:

> We're concerned about parents who carry on their shoulders the entire burden for their kids' salvation and lifelong happiness. We were never meant to carry the ultimate responsibility for anyone's soul: neither our own nor our children's. Only the Good Shepherd is strong enough to carry a soul—that's his job, not ours.[3]

Salvation is the work of the Lord. So when we take credit for what is going on in our children's lives, we are stealing glory from God.

This works for the flip side of the equation also. If we find our identity in how our children act, we could be utterly devastated if they end up not serving the Lord. We could walk around believing that we are unloved failures. We become parents with bad kids instead of children of God. Finding our identity in anything our children do, good or bad, will lead to either pride or despair. Which is once again why I am calling you back to living in your identity as a child of our heavenly Father—loved, carried, fed, protected, disciplined, and never forgotten.

When we use our children to build our own identity, we cease to love them. We cannot simultaneously love and use someone. Using your son to build your ego because he is good at sports or using your daughter to make you feel good about yourself because she is pretty is idolatry of the worst form. You are essentially sacrificing your children to yourself. This is why the doctrine of adoption and the beauty of God as our Father are important. When your child fails to hit the home run, or your daughter doesn't dress in a way you believe flattering, or worse, your son ends up in jail or your daughter ends up pregnant, you can remember that *you* are not how your child performs. That is not your identity. So in those moments you can love without shame or anger. You can discipline and correct without flying off the handle, because the discipline will be about restoring *them* instead of regaining your identity. It will be for their good instead of a release for you. It will be a regaining of intimacy for the family instead of your holding them at arm's length and making them work their way back into your good graces. You and I will never do these things perfectly, but even in the midst of our anger and self-righteous arrogance, God is lovingly calling us to rest in him.

When we see how little we deserve to be called "children of God" and how extravagant his grace is in calling us his beloved sons and daughters, we can extend that same grace to our children. They will sin against us, but the deeper we press into his love, the more their sin will be grievous because it is against him and the less it will be about how they disrespected us.

Our children will need discipline. They need to be trained and corrected, but always in the context of love. We cannot and should not expect our children to obey perfectly. *We* don't even do that. There are times when we deal self-righteously with our children, when we act shocked by their sin of selfishness or anger. Ironically, we have probably been selfish and angry that very day ourselves. Instead of coming at them like someone who never sins, we can shoulder the sorrow of sin with them as fellow sinners in desperate need of a Savior. The Bible tells us in Romans 3:10: "There is none righteous, no, not one" (KJV). If we know this to be true, why do we expect our children to behave in a way that we can't even live up to?

I am not saying that we should not have rules. We absolutely should. It would be unloving to let our children do whatever they want. But when we see how God has loved us and chosen us and gently dealt with us despite our constant rebellion, how can we be distant from our kids when they disobey? We want to protect ourselves from being hurt by them, but this is never how God treats us. I do not say these things to shame you, but rather to encourage you to lift your eyes up to him. In those times when your children don't love you back, or they spurn the wisdom you want to share with them, you can remember that God was a strong enough Father to make you his child. He can do the same for them.

Of the Lord

> Fathers, do not provoke your children to anger, but bring them up in the discipline and instruction of the Lord.
>
> Ephesians 6:4

> Fathers, do not provoke your children, lest they become discouraged.
>
> Colossians 3:21

These two mirroring verses are actually the only two commands to parents in the entire New Testament. In them, most of us, at first glance, see a command to dads to be careful not to anger their kids and to raise them with discipline and teaching. A myriad of books has been written on what *discipline and instruction, bring them up,* and *provoke* mean.

But we have focused on the wrong parts of these verses. We have solely focused on what *we* are to do and forgotten what Jesus is about and what *he* has done. Without "of the Lord" at the end of Ephesians 6:4, we would have no good news to give to our children. They would have no motivation for obedience, and we would miss out on sharing the joy of the gospel of Jesus with them.

The three words "*of the Lord*" would have been revolutionary to the early readers in Ephesus. The Greeks in the city would have brought their children up in the discipline and instruction of the philosophers of the day. With Socrates, Aristotle, and Plato leading the pack of great thinkers, the Greeks would have prized their wisdom and taught their children to do the same. Modern-day pop psychology is our equivalent of the accepted wisdom of the day, with proponents such as Dr. Spock, Dr. Phil, and maybe even Oprah. (Poor comparisons to the Greek philosophers, I know.)

These same three words would have shocked the Jews who received the letter from Paul. They would have brought their children up in the discipline and instruction of the Law. The Torah was the rule of the day, and fathers spent their time learning it and training their children in it.

This is where the majority of the church is today. We want our kids to behave, so we spend the bulk of our time trying to get kids to simply know and follow the rules. Too often we forget about their hearts.

To train our children in the Lord is gospel-centered parenting. We are instructed to tell them about Jesus' life, death, resurrection, ascension, and his intercession for them. We must tell them the good news of all that salvation brings: full forgiveness, adoption, redemption, atonement, and propitiation (Romans 3:25; 1 John 2:2).

You don't have to use all those big, delicious theological words with your kids, but you can break them down into words they understand and illustrate them with everyday situations. For example,

- When your child lies because he doesn't want to get into trouble, you can tell him that his life is hidden in Christ and the very sin he is trying to cover up has already been paid for (Colossians 3:3).
- When your child steals, you can tell her that God promises to take care of his kids and give them everything they need (Matthew 6:25–33).
- When your child feels alone, you can give the comforting words of Christ, "I am with you always, to the end of the age" (Matthew 28:20).
- When your child is troubled by his sin, you can tell him, "As far as the east is from the west, so far does he remove our transgressions from us" (Psalm 103:12).
- When your child feels friendless, you can tell her that Jesus calls us his friends (John 15:15).
- When your child feels like no one understands, share that Jesus sympathizes with him in his weakness, and Jesus prays for him with understanding of what he's going through (Hebrews 4:15).

Good News

The gospel really does change everything about our lives—the good news is just that! It is good news that informs each situation we encounter. As you share these truths with your children, you can know that the Holy Spirit's job is to open up their hearts to the beauty of it. Your job is to share; his job is to change. You can rest, you can enjoy your kids, and you can pray that the Holy Spirit will open their eyes and that he will use you in their lives.

The good news for us parents is that Jesus is strong and faithful enough to use our failures to glorify him. He works in our weaknesses and he proves himself strong.

Here is the good news for every parent who has failed their child, who has been angry, who has been impatient, who has been cold:

> He does not deal with us according to our sins, nor repay us according to our iniquities. For as high as the heavens are above the earth, so great is his steadfast love toward those who fear him; as far as the east is from the west, so far does he remove our transgressions from us. *As a father shows compassion to his children, so the Lord shows compassion to those who fear him.*
>
> Psalm 103:10–13, emphasis mine

Share that remarkable good news with your children when they are in the midst of sinning against you. Bring them to the cross and show them their need for a Savior.

5

Jesus Our Friend
and Our Friendships

Will You Be My Friend?

I remember in middle school passing a note to a girl in class that said, "Do you want to be my friend? Circle one, Yes or No." While I don't remember her answer, I do remember the feeling of wondering what she would say. In some ways, I still experience that same feeling as an adult when I meet someone for the first time. Are you familiar with the awkwardness of meeting someone you really enjoy and thinking that it was the start of a beautiful friendship, only to find out that they did not feel the same way? I will be honest, that is one of my biggest fears. I hate to be vulnerable and put my heart out there, not knowing if my feelings will be returned. I want to make absolutely sure that the feeling of friendship is reciprocated before I ever take that risk.

This chapter is a going to be a difficult one for me to write because I struggle in this area. That doesn't mean I don't have any friends. But rather that I have found my identity in my friendships for years. For as long as I can remember, really. I didn't experience much heartache in the area of boyfriends growing up because I have been with the same boy since I was fifteen. He has always been overwhelmingly kind and gracious and never really hurt me. And so maybe it was because I knew I always had him that I tried hard to improve my righteousness, okay-ness, or identity by having the "right" friends around me. I think this is a common struggle for women. I know that every time I speak on friendship, women from teenagers to grandmothers come up to me and tell me they have felt the same way.

I am sure there are plenty of books out there that tell you how to be a better friend or how to choose good, godly friends. I've often read books like that before in order to be the best friend anybody ever had, not because I loved them but because I wanted that to be my reputation. Ugly, I know. So I don't plan on giving you the ten steps to being a great friend in this chapter. You are probably picking up on a theme with that one. And after what I have told you about myself, you are most likely breathing a sigh of relief.

Chances are we have either deeply hurt our friends, been deeply hurt *by* friends, or have experienced the hurt of feeling friendless. Let's be honest, we are all pretty much horrible at being friends. We are, by nature, bent in on ourselves and always looking for ways to please ourselves, which is the mortal enemy of true friendship. There are times that even our best deeds or our kindest actions toward our friends are really done with ourselves in mind. As with my example earlier, I wanted to be a good friend so that others would think highly of me. Have you ever done something nice for someone all the while anticipating a compliment in return? Now, don't get me wrong. I am not saying that every single time we do something nice it is completely for ourselves, but what I *am* saying is that this self-serving can sneak into our relationships very easily, and at times we aren't even aware of it.

As we start to understand friendship a little bit better, let's start by looking upward instead of inward. Instead of telling you how to improve as a friend, I want to lift your eyes from yourself to see how the Creator of the universe has befriended you. I am convinced that the more we dwell on how he has been our friend, the more we will find ourselves being the friends we are called to be.

God and Abraham: BFFs

God initiates friendship with his people. Read that sentence again. It should absolutely blow your mind. God initiates friendship. God calls us (the church, the offspring of Abraham) his friend in Isaiah 41:8–10 (emphasis mine):

> But you, Israel, my servant, Jacob, whom I have chosen, *the offspring of Abraham, my friend*; you whom I took from the ends of the earth, and called from its farthest corners, saying to you, "You are my servant, I have chosen you and not cast you off"; fear not, for I am with you; be not dismayed, for I am your God; I will strengthen you, I will help you, I will uphold you with my righteous right hand.

What does God promise in this relationship of friendship with us? He promises that he is with us and we don't need to fear. We don't need to be dismayed because he is our God. That word *dismayed* means "to anxiously look about." Have you ever felt that way in a social gathering? Wondering whom you should talk to or what you should do? God calling you his friend directly speaks to that. We don't have to anxiously wonder whom we should befriend, because God is our God. He promises to strengthen, help, and uphold us. His friendship gives us confidence to love others.

He Believed

What did Abraham do (or what do we have to do) in order to be called God's friend? We can look to James 2:23 to answer that question: "The Scripture was fulfilled that says, 'Abraham believed God, and it was counted to him as righteousness'—and he was called a friend of God." All Abraham did was believe. The faith to believe comes from God. "For by grace you have been saved through faith. And this is not your own doing; it is the gift of God" (Ephesians 2:8). Here we see God both initiating friendship and giving us everything we need to enter into the friendship.

Have you ever seen someone you know you should be nice to but you really don't like? It almost hurts your soul to be around them, but you feel obligated. So you just tell yourself it will only be for a little bit and then you force yourself to go talk to them. This is never God's disposition toward us. He doesn't feel obligated to be our friend; it is his joy to be in relationship with us. I know I need the Holy Spirit to convince me of this truth.

In my life, if someone wants to be my friend, they have to do a lot more than believe I want to be theirs. I make others live under my covenant of works. If you continue to be the friend I desire, then I will be your friend. The demands that I have placed on friends are ridiculous and unattainable. I have asked them to always be there for me. I have asked them to cheer me up when I am down. I have asked them to think of me continually. Now I have never actually said those things to them, but I have certainly been disappointed when they have not done those things for me. And yet, the very thing I am looking for them to do has already been done by Jesus Christ. He cares for me, prays for me, and loves me at every moment of every day.

Jesus Calls You His Friend

> Love one another the way I loved you. This is the very best way to love. Put your life on the line for your friends. You are my friends when you do the things I command you. I'm no longer calling you servants because servants don't understand what their master is thinking and planning. No, I've named you friends because I've let you in on everything I've heard from the Father.
> You didn't choose me, remember; I chose you, and put you in the world to bear fruit, fruit that won't spoil. As fruit bearers, whatever you ask the Father in relation to me, he gives you.
> But remember the root command: Love one another.
>
> John 15:12–17 The Message

Not only do we have the great and unexplainable privilege of being called God's friend, we also now see Jesus make the same proclamation over us. This passage is from John 15. Jesus is at the Last Supper with his disciples and he is trying to prepare them for what is about to happen to him. He essentially tells them he is going to prove his love by laying down his life for them. I am sure the disciples don't understand all the implications of what Jesus is saying here. Truth be told, I don't think we can fully grasp it either. But we do hear this word of pursuing, life-giving love. Jesus sits with his disciples and says, "I am about to show you what the greatest love in the world looks like." What I believe makes this even lovelier is that they don't fully grasp it. Can you imagine the conversations they had after the crucifixion?

"Remember when he said that there was no greater love than a man who lays down his life for his friends? He was talking about how he felt about *us*." The joy, the awe, the sheer shock that he was telling them what was about to happen was probably overwhelming. The Holy Spirit must have reminded them of that sentence at just the right moment. And for you and me, that is exactly how he feels about us too. There is no greater love. May the Holy Spirit remind us of this beautiful truth daily, hourly.

Obedience = Friendship?

Right after this proclamation of friendship, Jesus tells his disciples, "You are my friends if you do what I command you." This seems to fly in the face of everything I have said up to this point. It seems to be saying that he will be our friend only if we obey. But that isn't what Jesus is saying at all. His friendship came first. "This obedience is not what *makes* them friends; it is what *characterizes* his friends."[1] I have lived most of my life under the assumption that if I am not obeying, then Christ doesn't want any part of me. That is a terrible weight and it is a lie. God's love for us in Christ always precedes our loveliness. His faithfulness always precedes ours, and his friendship is what brings us into relationship with him. Think of the story of *Beauty and the Beast*. Before the Beast turned into the handsome prince, Beauty loved him. In fact, it was her love that transformed him. She loved him before he was lovely. Now the analogy breaks down because Beast was actually a cute prince to begin with, but we aren't. We were enemies of God when he first set his affection on us.

If we are true believers of Christ, we will obey. That doesn't mean we will obey perfectly. It doesn't even mean we will obey nine times out of ten. But it does mean that we will have a desire to obey. If your life is characterized by a growing desire to obey, you can be sure that you are a friend of Jesus. It is his very pronouncement of "my friend" that gives us the longing to be obedient to his commands. His love for us is what engenders a heart of obedience. There will be days where you have a special grace and you find obedience easy and a joy. And there will be days where you feel like you don't even know what obedience would look like. On either day, you must remember that your obedience or disobedience doesn't merit anything from God anymore. Being obedient will obviously lead to a better life for us. God has given us rules for living so we can know how to enjoy him and life the most. Obedience should be what we strive for and long for. But on our days of disobedience, we can remember that Christ knows our weaknesses and sympathizes with us in them. On our days of obedience we can remember that even the desire to obey and the ability to obey come from him alone. "The radical grace of the gospel transforms servanthood into friendship. Only grace can free us to obey Jesus out of friendship and worship, and no longer out of fear or self-interest."[2]

No Servants/No Secrets

"No longer do I call you servants, for the servant does not know what his master is doing; but I have called you friends, for all that I have heard from my Father I have made known to you" (John 15:15). Christ reiterates again that he thinks of us as friends, not as servants. Interesting that he says this right after the sentence about obedience. He knows that our hearts will go to the call for obedience and then retreat into a servant-master relationship versus the friendship he is calling us into. When we think he is disappointed in us for not producing the way we should, we can be sure we are still stuck in the servant-master mind-set. When we feel as though we can never please God because we have failed so many times, we are stuck in that old mind-set. When we are afraid of what he thinks of us because we haven't had our quiet time for the day, we are bogged down with wrong thinking. We no longer have to work to earn God's favor. Jesus Christ did the work, completely. We have a different relationship now—one of friendship, one of love, one of understanding.

Christ doesn't invite us into friendship and then keep us at arm's length. He tells us that he wants to share everything he knows from the Father with us. He invites us in completely, with no hesitation, no conditions, no judgments, just pure welcome. Relationship with God is the ultimate goal of Christianity. This relationship is not something we can do; it is something that has happened to us. Jesus isn't satisfied with our just calling him Master or Lord. He desires more for us. It is inconceivable that he, the truest of friends, would want to be in relationship with me, the most unfaithful. John Calvin wrote, "Those hearts must be harder than iron or stone which are not softened by such incomparable sweetness of divine love."[3]

What we deserve, at the very best, is to be called a servant. This was what the prodigal son asked for. He wanted to prove himself, to work for a relationship. Our God, like the father of the prodigal, will have nothing to do with that. When we come face-to-face with what we are, it feels like too much to even ask God—our heavenly Father—if we can be a servant! The heart of the Father is to offer us something much better: "I don't want you as servants. I call you friends."

I Chose You

As if his previous words weren't enough, Jesus condescends even further and tells us, "You did not choose me, but I chose you and appointed you that you should go and bear fruit and that your fruit should abide, so that whatever you ask the Father in my name, he may give it to you" (John 15:16). I love his heart right here. He doesn't shame us for not choosing him; he just comes right out and says, "Even though I am not your choice, you are mine." We don't have to ever think that the basis of our friendship is our desire for it. It is not based on our goodness or our great decision to follow after him. He chose us.

Not only did he choose us, but he also gave us a confident reminder that in every way he has appointed us to bear fruit, we can be sure we will bear that fruit. "For we are his workmanship, created in Christ Jesus for good works, which God prepared beforehand, *that we should walk in them*" (Ephesians 2:10, emphasis mine). So many times you and I walk around fearfully, wondering if we are doing enough or if we are doing it in the right way. The answer to our questions is that we won't ever do it completely right. We aren't Jesus, and we won't ever be able to do enough to pay God back for what he has done for us. Actually, he doesn't want us to pay him back! He is so generous that he tells us he has already prepared what he wants us to do, and we will accomplish those good works. He has appointed us to bear fruit. It will blossom. That fills my heart with so much joy. I don't need to be afraid of failing. He has our entire lives in the palm of his hands. He has it all.

As if that generosity and kindness were not enough, he then goes on to tell us that we need to believe the Father's heart for his children. Ask him. Jesus encourages us to pray. The way he does this is by reminding us what God is about. He is about giving good gifts to his kids. My husband is the best gift giver around. I don't know how he always knows what to get our kids, but he just does. My oldest son once said of him, "He knows what I want better than I know. He always gets me what I would have asked for if I would've known what he knows." My husband gets such joy from watching our kids react to the presents he gives them. Christmas morning is his favorite time of the year, because he loves to see them excited and happy. This is a picture of how God is with us every single day. He is telling us that if we feel like we can't bear fruit, we are able to ask the Father to help us by giving us everything we need to bear the fruit he has promised. If we are in a situation where the bearing of fruit is painful, we can rest assured that this is a process our Father has ordained and he will carry us through it. Jesus tells us to ask in his name. It is as if he is saying, "If you feel like you can't ask, just tell the Father you are with me." Now this isn't because God forgets we are his children. It is for our own benefit. It is to remind us that we are in Christ. That all the blessings he earned are now ours. We build faith in our hearts when we pray "in Jesus' name."

Now Love Each Other

After Jesus reassures us of his love and of the Father's help, he then commands us to "love one another" (John 15:17). You see, it is because of his love that we are able to love each other. Because of his announcement that he is our friend, I am able to love my friends. The lovely truth about dwelling on his proclamation of "friend" over me is that it frees me up to be a true friend to those around me. No longer am I looking to get into the "in" crowd; *Jesus* has called me his friend! No longer do I have to wonder if others reciprocate my feelings; Jesus has loved me eternally even when I don't love him in return! No longer do I need to worry about whether or not a friend is meeting my needs; Jesus is truly all the friend I need! No longer do I have to demand that my friends are always available to walk me through a situation;

Jesus never leaves my side! No longer do I have to make others prove that they're worthy of my love; when I was unlovely and unworthy, God initiated and now sustains a relationship with me.

My Savior has proved his love and friendship by laying down his life for me. This opens up my heart and allows me to lay down my life for others. He has loved me when I don't deserve it, even when I forget him. This changes my friendships; I can love even when I don't feel like I am being treated the way I deserve.

I shared with a friend that I was writing a chapter on friendship, and she said it should actually be a chapter on forgiveness. This is so true. Part of being a friend is the inevitability of being sinned against and sinning against others. Christ's friendship toward us is the only friendship that is guaranteed to be pain-free. Jesus will never disappoint us or hurt us by sinning against us. We *will* be hurt by others (and others *will* be hurt by us). It is just a fact. But we can learn to love through the pain because he experienced the greatest pain in history to love us. C. S. Lewis puts it this way:

> To love at all is to be vulnerable. Love anything, and your heart will certainly be wrung and possibly be broken. If you want to make sure of keeping it intact, you must give your heart to no one, not even to an animal. Wrap it carefully round with hobbies and little luxuries; avoid all entanglements; lock it up safe in the casket or coffin of your selfishness. But in that casket—safe, dark, motionless, airless—it will change. It will not be broken; it will become unbreakable, impenetrable, irredeemable.[4]

You Be Jesus . . . No, Wait, I Will Be Jesus

We often expect our friends to be Jesus. We want them to understand us completely. We want them to always be available.

We want them to hear us perfectly. We want them to love us unconditionally. All of these things are roles reserved exclusively for our Savior.

There are also times when we want to be Jesus for our friends. We want them to view us as never making a mistake or hurting them. And when they accuse us of hurting them, we look for all sorts of reasons to insist it wasn't our fault. We want to be the only one they turn to for help. When they look to others, we feel like they are being unfaithful to us. We want them to be fully aware of what an incredible friend we are, and when they don't seem to grasp the magnitude of our greatness, we are sullen and withhold affection.

There is one Messiah, and you and I are not him, and we shouldn't expect our friends to be our Messiah either.

How to Kill a Friendship

Whenever we find our identity in anything other than our oneness with Christ, we will kill the false identity maker. When we use friendship to find identity, we will strangle the friendship. In essence, we are asking that friendship to give us something that God in Christ alone can give. "For natural loves that are allowed to become gods do not remain loves. They are still called so, but can become in fact complicated forms of hatred."[5]

Let me explain what I mean here. When I make a certain friendship into an idol in my life, I am expecting that person to be my savior. When they don't live up to my expectations (and they won't because they can't), I will end up hating them for not fulfilling my needs. Expectations are the very root of bitterness. We all have different expectations we place on friends—maybe it is to text us during the day, invite us to a meal, or remember our birthday. When our friend doesn't meet those expectations, we become angry or sad, or feel unloved. That is fertile soil for bitterness. Essentially, we are saying, "I know how to be a better friend than you do. Therefore, I am a better person than you are." Self-righteousness at its nasty height.

A close ally of expectations is judgment. When you don't behave the way I deem appropriate, I will judge you. Once I have sentenced you to the prison of "You don't meet my expectations," the friendship will suffer. I often will take something a friend has done and ascribe motives to it. If a friend doesn't come up and give me a hug at church, then suddenly, in my mind, they are angry with me and don't care about me anymore. I will then act differently toward them because I feel as though things have changed. They in turn will feel my coldness and retreat. I know this sounds like a silly scenario, but I can almost guarantee it happens every single Sunday.

Being self-occupied kills a friendship. If a friend doesn't love you the way you feel you should be loved, your self-interest suffocates whatever love was there. Often we are friends with people who are the opposite of us. My dear friend Kei loves to be alone. One of her favorite things to do is to go to the beach, by herself, to sit and read. Now, one of my favorite things to do is to go to the beach with my friend. I love to sit and read with her next to me. But when I hear that she has gone to the beach without me, I can either assume she means she doesn't want to be with me, or I can look beyond myself and see I am not the only person in this friendship. There are actually two of us and we both have different desires and different personalities. There must be room in our friendships to be different people. We must allow our friends to be the way they have been created.

Trying to fix a friend is another great way to kill a friendship. It is painful for us to sit with a friend who is hurting, whether their pain is due to their own sin or someone else's, and just be with them. We want to fix them. We hate seeing reminders of our own brokenness. That is why when a friend comes to you with a problem in her life, your first instinct is to help her see where she went wrong and try to correct the situation.

One of the hardest things to do as a friend is to "weep with those who weep." Now, I am not saying we should never offer advice to our friends; there is a time and a place for that. But can we learn to listen first without trying to fix? Can we stop and grieve with a friend without trying to get through the problem quickly? Henri Nouwen powerfully said,

> When we honestly ask ourselves which persons in our lives mean the most to us, we often find that it is those who, instead of giving much advice, solutions, or cures, have chosen rather to share our pain and touch our wounds with a gentle and tender hand. The friend who can be silent with us in a moment of despair or confusion, who can stay with us in an hour of grief and bereavement, who can tolerate not-knowing, not-curing, not-healing and face with us the reality of our powerlessness, that is the friend who cares.[6]

It is in the hurt and the confusion that we learn to love selflessly. We learn in those situations that we aren't Jesus. That we can't just make it all better, that this world is broken, and hurt is prevalent. It is painful to stop and stay with a friend in their hurt. We hate feeling helpless. We have far too high an opinion of ourselves. We think if we can just dispense the right advice and our friend would just obey our words, everything would be okay.

The irony here is that you too have had the right advice given. The Bible is full of it, but you can't follow it perfectly and you are broken. We hate seeing the ugliness of our brokenness, which is why it is so hard to sit with a friend in the middle of their hurt, especially if we believe they brought that hurt on themselves. In the sitting, we need to be reminded that we have a bedrock of a Savior, that he loves us right in the broken moments, in the middle of our confusion. That he in fact does understand everything we are going through. That he truly is our only hope in life and death. That even though, as my pastor says, "Our idols will always break our hearts," we have a Savior who is "near to the brokenhearted" (Psalm 34:18).

Not Just What I Want

> Let each of you look not only to his own interests, but also to the interests of others. Have this mind among yourselves, which is yours in Christ Jesus, who, though he was in the form of God, did not count equality with God a thing to be grasped, but emptied himself, by taking the form of a servant, being born in the likeness of men. And being found in human form, he humbled himself by becoming obedient to the point of death, even death on a cross.
>
> Philippians 2:4-8

This is a perfect verse to remember for any relationship. Paul tells us to have the mind that is already ours. You are already one with Christ; he is your friend. He lived as a servant, looking out for what everybody else wanted. I know I am incapable of doing this perfectly. And quite honestly, on the days I try and sort of succeed, I am wrapped up in how awesome I am. That is why it is so amazing that he took his love all the way to death, even death on a cross. As he died on the cross for our sins and was resurrected for our justification, he gave us this mind-set. We are now able to live looking out for other people. We don't have to feel like our interests or the ways we show friendship are the best and only ways; we don't have to fight to be loved.

We have already been loved completely unselfishly. The more I am aware of this love, the more I will be able to love others.

The grace he has extended to me changes me. It changes my friendships. I would love to tell you that I never struggle because I remember his friendship all the time. Honestly, I do struggle, and at times I don't even try— I just give in to the jealousy and the idolatry. But in the midst of those times, the Holy Spirit reminds me that this friendship with God is an unrelenting friendship. It comes to me, it chooses me, it doesn't let me go.

Forgiveness for the Unfriendly

You may read this chapter and feel as though you are an awful friend and will never be able to be anything but an awful friend. The really good news is that Jesus was accused of associating with sinners (Luke 15:2). Octavius Winslow says about that verse,

> Nothing gave greater offence to the scribes and Pharisees than the divine mission of Jesus to save sinners. No greater and more virulent accusation could they allege against Him, than that, He extended His compassionate regards to the vile and the wretched, admitting the most flagrant offenders to His mercy, and inviting the most notorious sinners to His fellowship. And yet this, His greatest reproach, was His highest honor. Pluck this jewel from His mediatorial crown, and it has lost its costliest gem. Extract this note from the "joyful sound," and you have hushed its sweetest melody. Remove this object of His mission from His coming, and you have reduced His incarnation, sufferings, and death to a gigantic waste.[7]

He truly loves sinners, so we can love them too. We can take our friends with all of their ugliness and we can love them because we have been loved.

We can look for the alienated and the isolated and we can befriend them. That is what we once were. You may feel isolated now, but I promise there are others in your community of believers who feel the exact same way. Look for those who are around you. Open your eyes to those who are hurting. Go beyond what you think you need and look for those who are in pain, remembering always that in every way you fail to be a friend, he has forgiven and loved you.

Beloved friends of Christ, may we never forget that all of the love and acceptance we look for in each other can be found only in the arms of Christ. His arms, once outstretched on the cross for us, remain outstretched, but now reach toward us.

6

God's Mission and Our Relationships With Our Communities

Are We Ashamed?

*T*here is a video on YouTube that went viral among Christians. It is of Penn Jillette, from Penn & Teller, talking about a man who proselytized him. Penn is an unashamed, outspoken atheist. In this video he tells the story of a man who approached him after one of his shows and gave him a Bible. The part that is a slap in the face is when Penn says,

> I don't respect people who don't proselytize. I don't respect that at all. If you believe that there is a heaven and hell, and people could be going to hell or not getting eternal life or whatever and you think, *Well, it is not really worth telling them this because it would make it socially awkward.* . . . How much do you have to hate somebody to not proselytize? How much do you have to hate somebody to believe that everlasting life is possible and not tell them that?[1]

This is a punch in the stomach of our embarrassing hesitancy to speak to our community about what we truly believe.

I don't know if it is a fear of being socially awkward, or if it is because we don't really know what to say, or if we are just lazy. There are probably a myriad of reasons why we don't share the gospel. I would venture to say one main reason is because we don't really think of it as good news. We aren't enraptured with the Father's heart toward us, his Son's generosity doesn't move us, and the Holy Spirit's ongoing and unending work doesn't stir our hearts. We aren't taken with the Father's mission.

We find it so easy to praise other things we love in front of people who don't hold the same viewpoint. For instance, I love the San Diego Padres. I mean I love, love them. Like almost an unhealthy, idolatrous love. I love talking about them, even to people who don't care about sports. I must bore 90 percent of my girlfriends when I talk about a game-winning hit (which rarely happens for us) or a beautifully pitched game (also very rare) or a play that took my breath away. I have zero problem telling people about my love. I even find delight in talking about the Padres when I know that my friend likes another MLB team. Now, I know that talking sports and talking about God and his love for us are different. I know that religion is a very sensitive topic for people. My point is, we talk about what we love. I believe that if our hearts were absorbed in the love of God through Christ's work for us, we would find it much easier to talk about him. My hope is that with this chapter I will build your love for how God loves the world.

Looking to Gather

From the very beginning of time, God has been looking to gather a people for himself. You can see his heartbeat in Genesis 17:7–8:

> And I will establish my covenant between me and you and your offspring after you throughout their generations for an everlasting covenant, to be God to you and to your offspring after you. And I will give to you and to your offspring after you the land of your sojournings, all the land of Canaan, for an everlasting possession, and I will be their God.

God was never looking to save one or two people and call it quits. He was always looking for generation after generation that would bear his name, eternally. We hear repeated over and over again his promise to be Israel's God and make them his people, his "treasured possession" (Deuteronomy 4:20; 7:6; 14:2; 26:18; Leviticus 26:11–12). In creating the world, God had a plan—he wanted a people.

The Mission Defined

Isaiah 61:1–3 explains how God is going to bring this people, this possession, to himself:

> The Spirit of the Lord God is upon me, because the Lord has anointed me to bring good news to the poor; he has sent me to bind up the brokenhearted, to proclaim liberty to the captives, and the opening of the prison to those who are bound; to proclaim the year of the Lord's favor, and the day of vengeance of our God; to comfort all who mourn; to grant to those who mourn in Zion—to give them a beautiful headdress instead of ashes, the oil of gladness instead of mourning, the garment of praise instead of a faint spirit; that they may be called oaks of righteousness, the planting of the Lord, *that he may be glorified* (emphasis mine).

I don't know if there is a clearer description of the gospel than what we just read. This is God's heart for his people. It is good news. He wants to see the brokenhearted healed, the captives set free, those in prison unbound, all those who are mourning comforted. When you think of sharing the gospel, is this what you think of? I know it isn't for me. I feel like I need to coerce someone into making a statement of belief in Jesus Christ. And while that is a part of the gospel, it isn't the whole thing. We tend to take this good news and turn it into a list of things that people have to do in order to go to heaven.

Our Hearts Are Far

God has a difficult work to do. How do you bind a broken heart when the heart is dead toward you? How do you set a captive free when they love their prison cell? This is what the Bible says about us before God enlivens our hearts. Titus 3:3 describes us as "foolish, disobedient, led astray, slaves to various passions and pleasures, passing our days in malice and envy, hated by others and hating one another." The apostle Paul puts it this way:

> They were filled with all manner of unrighteousness, evil, covetousness, malice. They are full of envy, murder, strife, deceit, maliciousness. They are gossips, slanderers, haters of God, insolent, haughty, boastful, inventors of evil, disobedient to parents, foolish, faithless, heartless, ruthless.
>
> Romans 1:29–31

If these two descriptions of those outside of Christ don't encompass what seething, hateful people we once were, I don't know what will.

These two descriptions compared to what God wants to do for us, and who we are, are at complete odds. It isn't as though we were helpless, brokenhearted *good* people who were looking for someone to come along and bind our wounds with their love. We were evil-encompassed haters of God. We actually loved our prison cells. So how do you free someone who doesn't want freedom?

He Takes the Initiative

God sent Jesus. He sent him to fulfill those verses we read in Isaiah 61, as quoted in Luke 4:18–19:

> The Spirit of the Lord is upon me, because he has anointed me to proclaim good news to the poor. He has sent me to proclaim liberty to the captives and recovering of sight to the blind, to set at liberty those who are oppressed, to proclaim the year of the Lord's favor.

After reading these words to the congregation in the synagogue in Nazareth, Jesus then proclaimed, "Today this Scripture has been fulfilled in your hearing" (Luke 4:21). By this declaration, Jesus revealed that this is his mission, this is his plan, and he will succeed. God loved the world so much that he sent Jesus to go get his people. The triune God working in complete harmony would set about to fulfill Isaiah 61. God would send Jesus by the power of the Holy Spirit to rescue a people that didn't want to be rescued. God "anointed" Jesus for this purpose. The Holy Spirit was "upon him" for this purpose. Primarily the gospel, the good news, is that Jesus has done all of these things for us. The gospel is how God has interacted with us, how he has rescued and redeemed us all, to gather a people unto himself for his own glory. What could be more beautiful than turning hate into love? What type of love must God have for his people that unbinds prisoners who love their chains?

Bring Good News to the Poor

The love revealed in these passages is such that God delights in coming to the poor, the afflicted, the imprisoned, and bringing them good news. Do you ever feel like you could just use some good news? There are days, weeks, months, possibly years where it feels as though all the news you hear is bad: children who have run away, unwed daughters pregnant, incurable diseases diagnosed, hard hearts, broken marriages, dying loved ones. In the midst of all the bad news, our loving heavenly Father sends Jesus to give us good news: "Listen, my beloved brothers, has not God chosen those who are poor in the world to be rich in faith and heirs of the kingdom, which he has promised to those who love him?" (James 2:5).

He has chosen the poor, who know they have nothing to offer and are aware of their need, and has proclaimed that they will be rich in him. We are close friends with a family that recently adopted a little girl from Uganda. The little girl did nothing to deserve it. She wasn't more likable than any of the other kids, or more beautiful than any of the other little girls. My friends just decided to place their affection on this little girl who had eaten only beans and rice every meal of her life, when she did eat. They decided to make her a part of their family and brought her home and made her rich. This is what God has done for us. He looks on us and loves us in our most miserably poor state and makes us rich—rich in the love that he bestows on us freely. God calls to us and says,

> Come, everyone who thirsts, come to the waters; and he who has no money, come, buy and eat! Come, buy wine and milk without money and without price. Why do you spend your money for that which is not bread, and your labor for that which does not satisfy? Listen diligently to me, and eat what is good, and delight

yourself in rich food. Incline your ear, and come to me; hear, that your soul may live; and I will make with you an everlasting covenant, my steadfast, sure love for David.

Isaiah 55:1–3

What does God ask us to do in these verses? Just admit to being poor and then receive the good news, that God loves those who don't have anything to offer. God isn't looking for you to pay him back for all that he has done. He gave you the gift of his Son, and you can never ever do enough good or give enough of anything to pay him back. All you can do is receive with a grateful heart. You can fall in love with him.

The world tells us only to give to those who are worthy, to give to those who can afford to pay you back. It is just how it works in school and business: You study and you get good grades; you perform well and you get a promotion; you prove that you have what it takes and people listen to you. The gospel is the opposite: Give to the unworthy, to those who could never pay you back. We are the poor. Knowing and believing that you are poor is actually good news. You can delight in your unworthiness because your poverty is what makes so much of God's generosity. If a rich man gives a large sum of money to one of his good friends who is also rich, we think, *Oh, that's fine, but he is probably expecting a favor in return.* If a rich man gives to a homeless man, the rich man's generosity is on full display. In the gospel, God's generosity is on full display.

Charles Spurgeon describes the poor in these verses like this:

You nobodies, you who have been turned upside down and emptied right out, you who are bankrupts and beggars, you who feel yourselves to be clothed with rags and covered with wounds and bruises and putrefying sores—you who are utterly

95

bad through and through and know it, and mourn it and are humbled about it—you may know that God has poured the holy oil without measure upon Christ on purpose that He might deal out mercy to such poor creatures as you are! What a blessing this is! How we ought to rejoice in the anointing of Jesus, since it benefits such despicable objects![2]

Until you embrace the poverty of your own heart, the good news will never seem all that good.

Bind up the Brokenhearted

We have a little saying around our house that we love to toss back and forth out of irony. When someone is doing something stupid and they get hurt, we say jokingly, "That's what you get." And although we are kidding around with each other, that current actually runs deep within our hearts. You do something dumb, you will probably get hurt, and if you are dumb enough to do something dumb, then . . . that is what you get. This is anti-gospel; it is contrary to the mission that God sent Jesus on. Most of the time when we are brokenhearted it is our own doing. I am not discounting the fact that we are sinned against and we experience real grief in this world. I am saying that a lot of our pain is a consequence of our idolatry. And yet, God does not come to us in our brokenheartedness and with a nonchalant shrug of the shoulders say, "That's what you get." He comes to us and binds up our hearts with cords of his unending love.

God describes himself as one who is "near to the brokenhearted and saves the crushed in spirit" (Psalm 34:18) and as one who "heals the brokenhearted and binds up their wounds" (Psalm 147:3). If there was ever one who understood what it is like to be brokenhearted, it is our Savior. It was part of the mission of

God. God was brokenhearted by sending his Son to die. Jesus was heartbroken on the cross as he cried out for the relationship with his Father that was broken.

I have a dear friend whose husband committed adultery. By the grace of God they are reconciled now. Through her experiencing that horrific event, among other things, God has given her a special compassion and understanding for women who are going through the same situation. She is able to bear other women's burdens in a way that I never could, since I haven't experienced that type of pain. She has felt the pain they are feeling; she knows every emotion and every heartache. In the same way, and actually even more so, because Jesus Christ was the only innocent sufferer in all of history, he understands what it is like to feel brokenhearted, and he knows how to bind our wounds. Octavius Winslow said,

> Never did a physician more delight to display his skill, or exercise the benevolent feelings of his nature in the alleviation of suffering, than does Jesus in his work of binding up, soothing and healing the heart broken for sin, by speaking a sense of pardon, and applying to it the balsam of his own most precious blood. But our Lord not only heals the contrite heart, but as if heaven had not sufficient attraction as his dwelling-place, he comes down to earth and makes that heart his abode: "Thus says the Lord, To this man will I look, even to him that is poor and of a contrite spirit, and trembles at my word." And again, "Thus says the high and lofty One that inhabits eternity, whose name is Holy, I dwell in the high and holy place, with him also who is of a contrite and humble spirit, to revive the spirit of the humble, and to revive the heart of the contrite ones."[3]

Proclaiming Liberty and Opening Cell Doors

In 1987, Michael Morton was convicted of beating his wife to death. He proclaimed his innocence throughout the trial, and although there was never any physical evidence tying him to the murder scene, he was convicted and sent to prison. Mr. Morton spent nearly twenty-five years in prison before he was released due to DNA evidence. He had wasted almost a quarter of a century in a jail cell for a crime he was unjustly convicted of. The joy and relief of being released, of starting his life over again, of spending time with his son who was three when his mother died, is an emotion that most of us will never understand. Michael Morton didn't deserve to be in prison and he didn't want to be there. He and his lawyers waged a twenty-five-year fight to free him.

An innocent man punished for the sins of the guilty? Sound familiar? The difference is that Morton was freed. He ended up being exonerated because he wasn't guilty. Jesus Christ was willingly punished so that he could free the guilty. It almost seems scandalous. Opening the prison doors for the guilty? Proclaiming liberty to those who are bound? We deserve our prisons; we are the guilty. We have committed enough sin to condemn us to an eternity's worth of suffering and imprisonment, and yet the grace of God appears to those in prison, to those bound by their sin, and proclaims freedom. This grace and forgiveness shouts into our dungeons, "There is therefore now no condemnation for those who are in Christ Jesus" (Romans 8:1), and with that proclamation the chains fall off and the prison doors swing open.

What love, what joy, what peace should be ours when we think that we are free men and women. We are no longer bound to our sin, nor the judgment that our sin brings. How much more happiness and delight should we feel than Michael Morton? We don't deserve to be free. Our innocence was nonexistent, and yet we are freed from the eternal obligation to pay for our sins. Jesus has done it all. Praise him! And while we rejoice in this for ourselves, how often do we wish that others would get what they deserve?

"Do the crime, pay the time." We want justice, unless of course it is for our own wrongs. Then we want mercy. Christ's mission was to come and do the time for every single one of our crimes so that we could feel the sunshine of freedom every day of our lives.

Proclaiming the Year of the Lord's Favor

So now the prisoners are on the loose. We have been forgiven of our debt. Often we feel like now is the time to prove we are worth the work it took for God to free us. It is as if we think, *Okay, he got me out. Now I need to show him that was a good decision.* But before we get a chance to do that, we hear the word of the Lord's favor. He already favors us; we are already in his good graces. Second Corinthians 6:2 says, "Behold, now is the favorable time; behold, now is the day of salvation." We don't have to wait. God calls to us as we blindly stumble from our prison cells with broken hearts and not a penny of goodness to our names, and he says, "Now is the day of salvation." This is your testimony; this is my testimony—we don't have to wait to be saved.

"Come, Ye Sinners, Poor and Needy," by Joseph Hart, penned in 1759, says it perfectly:

> Come, ye sinners, poor and needy,
> Weak and wounded, sick and sore;
> Jesus ready stands to save you,
> Full of pity, love and power.
> I will arise and go to Jesus,
> He will embrace me in His arms;
> In the arms of my dear Savior,
> Oh, there are ten thousand charms.
> Come, ye thirsty, come, and welcome,
> God's free bounty glorify;

> True belief and true repentance,
> Every grace that brings you nigh.
> Come, ye weary, heavy laden,
> Lost and ruined by the fall;
> *If you tarry till you're better,*
> *You will never come at all* (emphasis mine).

We don't have to wait until we are better. Coming when you are better isn't actually coming to Jesus on his terms anyway. He is the one who cleans us; we don't need to come to him clean. We receive his grace immediately. There isn't a trial period where he waits on us to prove ourselves. We are right now, and right this minute, the Lord's favored. Seems hard to believe, doesn't it? I know it does for me. When I think about how I have lived this past week—how I have lied, how I have sought to make people praise me, how I have ignored my Bible reading, how my prayer life has been lacking—all these things and more should disqualify me from his favor, and yet by his grace I rest under his smile.

The Day of Vengeance Is Now

God is working right now to bring vengeance on all of his enemies. Although it may seem like sin, sorrow, and sickness have the upper hand, the truth is that they have already lost. They lost the minute Jesus rose from the grave, triumphant. We live in this time where the reality of Satan's destiny is not fully realized and he still "prowls around like a roaring lion, seeking someone to devour" (1 Peter 5:8). But our promise is that "after you have suffered a little while, the God of all grace, who has called you to his eternal glory in Christ, will himself restore, confirm, strengthen, and establish you" (1 Peter 5:10). What we see right now and experience right now is not the end of this battle. God promises that he will destroy the evil one and take care of each of his children in a personal, intimate way: "restore, confirm, strengthen, and establish." We do experience pain now, but he is coming back to make it all right.

To Comfort All Who Mourn

Once again, we see the tenderness of God's mission. It is almost as if he wants to tell us in as many ways as possible that he gets our pain. He wants to comfort us, give us gladness, and help us to see that we can praise. He calls us righteous. Truthfully, it is the declaration in Isaiah 61:3 that "they may be called oaks of righteousness, the planting of the Lord, that he may be glorified" that dries our tears and gives us reason to praise. Has he not seen every tear that we have cried? "You have kept count of my tossings; put my tears in your bottle. Are they not in your book?" (Psalm 56:8). What tenderness is this? When we feel like no one knows or sees our pain, there is One who keeps track of our tossings. It is almost too much love to understand. Isolation and loneliness add to our pain, and here is our Savior reminding us that we are not alone; we are never alone. Octavius Winslow says this: "The sigh that bursts in secret from my heart is not secret to Him; the tear that is my food day and night, and drops unperceived and unknown, is known and remembered by Him."[4] The mere thought that he sees and knows makes my sufferings and sadness seem a little more bearable. I am not alone in my trials. I have a faithful and ever-present help in times of trouble (Psalm 46:1).

This Mission and Our Cities

Our hearts should be overwhelmed with the beauty of this mission of God. The sympathy with which he reaches into our misery is a beauty unmatched. As we contemplate what Jesus was sent to do and actually did completely fulfill while he was here on earth, we should share this amazing good news with our neighbors.

There are lots of good books out there that delve into the topic of "how to" in a much deeper fashion than I am about to. However, one book I would heartily recommend is *Total Church: A Radical Reshaping Around Gospel and Community* by Tim Chester and Steve Timmis.

First, let me say I don't think there is one right way to do this. I think that God has gifted us all differently and uses us all uniquely. I can share with you my personal experience in this area, but I ask that you don't take it as the best or only way. The beautiful thing about the body of Christ is that we are a body, and each part has a different function.

I have found that in my life the easiest way to be on mission with God is to be a friend. I know that isn't revolutionary by any stretch of the imagination, but it is effective. People are lonely. Inviting someone to go for a walk or out for coffee or to a Fourth of July celebration is a very easy way to build relationship. You might be thinking, *What in the world would I talk to them about?* People love to talk about themselves. I mean, they absolutely love it. So all you have to do is ask questions. More often than not, question-asking will get deep into a person's life very quickly. If someone doesn't want to talk about himself, then you keep it general. Where do they work? How long have they lived in their house? Where did they live before that? Did they grow up religious? I used to be nervous about talking to people I didn't know until I realized I didn't have to get them signed up for church the next Sunday in one conversation. Friending people is a process; it is an investment.

Not only do you need to be interested in them, but you also must be willing to open up about yourself. Too often we like to portray ourselves as having it all together. When an unbelieving friend tells us about the way their child has acted, it isn't our job to act shocked. We aren't the keepers of morality. We don't have to look ashamed or disapproving of them when we walk up and find them smoking, swearing, or whatever. We remember that we were once in a jail cell just like them and our goodness didn't free us—*his* goodness did. We need to be willing to open up about our own mess-ups, to talk about how we have failed, and then if possible talk about how the love of Jesus has helped us or is helping us.

People often feel beaten down by those who are morally superior. Nobody wants to open up to someone they feel will judge them. The only way you won't exude judgment is to remember how you have been loved despite what you have deserved. We can take a fellow-prisoner approach versus a Christian-superstar approach. You are also going to have to be willing to hear their dirty laundry. This can be uncomfortable and at times disturbing. Entering into others' hurts with them is never tidy or convenient. You are going to have to be comfortable not knowing exactly what to say to someone. You are going to have to rely on the Holy Spirit to lead and guide.

In my experience, a very easy way to build friendship is through children. I love having all the neighbor kids think of my home as a safe and fun place to come and hang out. There are times when it is inconvenient to have loads of teenage boys in our apartment, but I want them to feel welcome. Once the kids are always over at our place, the parents are sure to follow. A simple conversation about dropping their son back off at their house can lead into inviting people over for lunch. If your children are involved in sports, a meal after a game at a local restaurant is an unassuming way to get to know someone.

His People/His Work

Now again, let me say that this is how my family has found it easy to get to know people. You may not have children, or maybe you don't like talking to people, but here is how I am sure that the Holy Spirit has a job. He was the one who enabled Jesus Christ to carry out the mission of God we have been looking at in this chapter. He will be the one who helps you carry out the same mission. You see it as *your* job, but it is *his* work that draws people and changes hearts. There is so much freedom in that, because you don't have to do it just right. He uses whatever means necessary to build his people.

You can't ignore the calling on your life to be about telling others the good news, but you can rest in his power to take people who were at one point not his and make them his. Jesus tells us in Matthew 28:19–20, "Go therefore and make disciples of all nations, baptizing them in the name of the Father and of the Son and of the Holy Spirit, teaching them to observe all that I have commanded you. And behold, I am with you always, to the end of the age." So often all we hear in those verses is what we should do, and we don't see the motivation given. Jesus promises to be with us, forever. He isn't sending us out to accomplish this mission without also promising that he is right by our side.

We can pray: pray for our cities, pray for our neighbors. My guess is that most of us don't ever even think about praying that opportunities would come up to share the good news and that we would also be given words to say. We can pray that our hearts will be soft to those suffering around us, that we will be able to see the hurting, lonely, confused prisoners that live next door. I don't say this to you as someone who has it all together, but as a fellow sinner who also needs to learn to pray. Oh, that our hearts would learn to love the way we have been loved! That we would look for the outcast and unpopular and show them what we have been shown.

The story that we hold closely to our hearts of being lost and now found is what we can live every day with our neighbors. We can look for practical, easy ways to love on them, and when the time comes, we can share how we have been healed and forgiven and favored.

Even in This We Are Forgiven

Are you ready for some good news? Even in this we are forgiven. In every way you fail to love your city and your community, Jesus loved perfectly on your behalf. Now, I am not saying that is a reason for laziness. I am saying that thought should fuel you to go beyond what you are comfortable with. It is not solely up to you to turn your neighborhood upside down, but who knows? God may use the fact that you gave your neighbor's kid a snack to show them his great love. I know that sounds simple—maybe too simple—but I have seen it. I have seen children's friendships turn entire families into families who know the love of God. God uses us. He loves using the weak and the confused, because then he gets all the glory. He even loves using the unwilling. He has used me when I was not only unwilling but also dreading being used. He is just that good and just that powerful.

7

God Our Husband and Our Marriages

The Whore and the Husband

Don't you love a great love story? A story where both parties are always and forever completely committed to each other no matter what the cost? Norma and Norman Burmah are the longest known married couple in the United States right now. They were married in 1931 and live in Louisiana. For eighty-three years they have given themselves to each other and remained faithful to their marriage vows. They attribute this longevity to trust, love, and attentiveness. Hearing about couples like this brings a smile to my face. We long for that type of love in our own lives. And while that is a good desire, the Burmahs aren't close to the greatest love story ever told.

Let me tell you a story about a man who was crazy in love with a woman. This man longed for this woman. He wanted to protect her. He wanted to cherish her. He delighted in her. He thought of her constantly and decided that she had to be his wife. Sounds beautiful, right? Now, let me tell you about the woman. She was . . . a whore. She didn't want to give herself to only one man. She loved the attention of multiple men. She didn't just love the attention, she loved the money and gifts the men she slept with gave to her. She knew she was loved exclusively and wholly by this one man, but she didn't care at all. He doted on her, gave her gifts, told her of his love, and she was indifferent.

Eventually, however, she gave in and became his wife. They committed to remaining faithful to each other. For him that was an eternal promise and a forever covenant. For her it was just words, like a thousand other words she had spoken previously and hadn't meant. After they were married for a bit, she decided she was bored and what she really needed was some of the excitement she had experienced before marriage. So she went back to her lifestyle of chasing men. She looked for other lovers, yes, lovers . . . plural. She longed for the gifts they gave her. She sold herself to her other lovers and was an actual sex slave for them.

From the day she left, her husband began searching for her, and when he finally found her, he had to pay for her in order to bring her home. From his own money and wealth he once again sacrificed for this woman who had little or no love for him. The man had *always* been faithful, regardless of her actions. Of course, his heart hurt because of what she had done. He threatened to punish and ignore, but in the end his love and his heart for this woman was so full and great that he took her back. He didn't just take her back reluctantly, though. He decided he would speak tenderly to her, allure her, woo her. He decided to give her gifts. He gave her hope that he would always love her. He asked her to call him her husband again. He had every right to take her outside the city gates and stone her, but instead he relinquished those rights. He literally owned her at this point, and yet he didn't want to be her master; he wanted to be intimate with her. He promised his steadfast love.

A story like this is stunning. We read about it and conclude that something is significantly wrong. He shouldn't love her after what she did to him. And if for some crazy reason he did decide to take her back, he should make *her* pay. He should be distant and remind her of all that she has done. He shouldn't be the one wooing her; she should have to work to woo him. She owes him big-time. It seems that his forgiveness of her is just enabling her to continue in her lifestyle—that essentially what he is communicating to her is "Just go ahead and do whatever you want. I will bail you out in the end." This story rubs us the wrong way. It doesn't fit into our quid pro quo philosophy: "I will love you to the degree that you love me." In our self-righteousness we can barely believe that anybody would be so dumb as to take a prostitute as a wife. It's crazy.

Here's the rub: You and I are that prostitute. Let that sink in for a minute.

Maybe you have guessed by now that the story above is from the book of Hosea. Hosea's marriage to Gomer is a parable illustrating God's relationship to his adulterous people (and by the way, we're "his adulterous people"). We play the role of the whore in this parable. Even writing that makes me a little angry. I don't want to view myself that way. I want to be the faithful one, the good one. And yet, the truth is that I am aware of God's unmatched love for me, of his good and plentiful gifts, and yet every day I run after other loves. What other loves? Instead of reading my Bible, I decide to spend some time on Facebook. Instead of believing that God's love is enough, I look for human approval and admiration. Instead of trusting that he will take care of me as he has promised to, I manipulate and worry and try to figure out ways to take care of myself. I am the adulterous spouse, and so are you.

How Sick Are Our Hearts?

Ezekiel 16 also has a lot to say about our idolatry, about our turning to other gods to find our happiness. It's easy to look at sin and shrug it off. I can think, *Well, that is not such a big deal. I mean, it was just a little lie, or a little gossip.* But every single time we put *anything* in God's place, we are committing adultery. It is no small matter. This is how God describes the condition of our hearts:

> How sick is your heart, declares the Lord God, because you did all these things, the deeds of a brazen prostitute, building your vaulted chamber at the head of every street, and making your lofty place in every square. Yet you were not like a prostitute, because you scorned payment. Adulterous wife, who receives strangers instead of her husband! Men give gifts to all prostitutes, but you gave your gifts to all your lovers, bribing them to come to you from every side with your whorings. So you were different from other women in your whorings. No one solicited you to play the whore, and you gave payment, while no payment was given to you; therefore you were different."
>
> Ezekiel 16:30–34

That is almost embarrassing to read. We would never consider ourselves *that* bad, and yet loving anything or anyone more than we love God is as disgusting as what is described in the verses above.

His Response to Our Sick Hearts

Hear, in contrast, these beautiful words for us:

> Therefore, behold, I will allure her, and bring her into the wilderness, and speak tenderly to her. And there I will give her her vineyards and make the Valley of Achor a door of hope. . . . And in that day, declares the Lord, you will call me "My Husband," and no longer will you call me "My Baal." . . . I will betroth you to me in righteousness and in justice, in steadfast love and in mercy. I will betroth you to me in faithfulness. And you shall know the Lord.
>
> Hosea 2:14–16, 19–20

He continues to speak of his faithfulness to us, even in the midst of our unfaithfulness. Throughout the book of Hosea we see threats of destruction for punishment. We see list after list of all the things Israel has done wrong. How God has longed to comfort them and be near to them and how they would have nothing to do with him. Then in 11:8 God says, "How can I give you up, O Ephraim? How can I hand you over, O Israel? . . . My heart recoils within me; my compassion grows warm and tender." In the very moment that God's anger at sin should be the controlling emotion, his heart can't do it. He feels compassion instead of anger. Unspeakable grace. He goes on to say, "I will not execute my burning anger; I will not again destroy Ephraim; for I am God and not a man, the Holy One in your midst, and I will not come in wrath" (v. 8). Wrath is what you and I deserve. He has every right to come after us with his full wrath on display, but he tells us, "I am not like you. I am God. That is not how I deal with my beloved." In fact he did have legitimate wrath that needed to be poured out on somebody. Praise him for sending his only Son to bear that wrath on our behalf so that we may forever know his love.

Our Maker Is Our Husband

Hosea and Ezekiel are not the only books in the Bible to use the imagery of a marriage between God and his people. Isaiah 54 also uses the covenantal language:

> For your Maker is your husband, the Lord of hosts is his name; and the Holy One of Israel is your Redeemer, the God of the whole earth he is called. For the Lord has called you like a wife deserted and grieved in spirit, like a wife of youth when she is cast off, says your God.

vv. 5–6

The affection he has for us just doesn't make sense humanly speaking:

> "With everlasting love I will have compassion on you." . . . "For the mountains may depart and the hills be removed, but my steadfast love shall not depart from you, and my covenant of peace shall not be removed," says the Lord, who has compassion on you.

vv. 8, 10

This is that love we have always longed for. This is how the Maker of the universe feels about us. To you and me, in our disobedience, in our stubbornness, in our sadness, in our anger, in our discontent, in our indifference, he tells us that nothing, absolutely nothing, will stop his love for us. Do you ever feel cast off? Do you ever feel deserted and grieved in spirit? Have you ever felt as though your past keeps him from really loving you, or maybe even your past keeps *you* from really loving *him*? The truth of the matter is that your past, whether pure or dirty, makes zero difference to him. He actually doesn't even see it. His forgiveness is complete. He is pursuing you, calling to you, gently wooing you, and longing for you to know that he loves you.

Costly Love

How can this be? How can a holy God betroth himself to a prostitute of a people? How can he, ultimate purity and light, mingle with dirtiness and darkness? It is only by the work that Jesus Christ has done for us. God doesn't look at the ugliness of our sin and turn a blind eye or excuse it. It must be dealt with or he would not be holy. So he does deal with our whorings. For every single time we have chased after other lovers, Jesus Christ took that sin on the cross. That sin was placed on his shoulders and he endured the wrath of God for our unfaithfulness. The Faithful One knew the pain of our unfaithfulness and he absorbed it completely. And all of God's threats to turn his back on an adulterous people were brought to fruition as God the Father turned his back on Jesus the Faithful One. All this pain so that we could become the bride who has been beautifully loved by the Holy Trinity. His love makes us lovely. It isn't because we are a beautiful bride that he loves us; it is because he chose to set his love on an adulterous people, and his love has changed us into a beautiful bride.

The Unfaithful Bride of Christ

Paul speaks about the unfaithfulness of the bride of Christ, the new Israel, the church, in 2 Corinthians 11:2–4:

> For I feel a divine jealousy for you, since I betrothed you to one husband, to present you as a pure virgin to Christ. But I am afraid that as the serpent deceived Eve by his cunning, your thoughts will be led astray from a sincere and pure devotion to Christ. For

113

if someone comes and proclaims another Jesus than the one we proclaimed, or if you receive a different spirit from the one you received, or if you accept a different gospel from the one you accepted, you put up with it readily enough.

The *ESV Gospel Transformation Bible* notes' perspective on these verses is excellent:

Christians understand themselves as betrothed to one husband (v. 2), awaiting the consummate marriage celebration at the bridegroom's return (Rev. 19:7–9). There is perhaps no greater illustration of gospel intimacy. God's deep and affectionate love for us moves us to worship, but it also reveals the darkness of our idolatry. . . . Though Paul wants to present the church as a pure virgin to Christ (2 Cor. 11:2), its people are deceived and defiled by false apostles. When God's redeemed people embrace other spirits, different gospels, and even a different Jesus (v. 4), they are committing adultery.

We ourselves commit spiritual adultery, and it's far more subtle than we think. When we fail to believe the gospel we not only suspect the truth and goodness of God; we place our faith in a different "good news." We ask something (or someone) to do what only the gospel is capable of doing.

What other "good news" do you sometimes believe? What other "husbands" captivate you? What other counterfeit hope captures your love? *The key to gospel fidelity is to know that Christ's sincere and pure devotion to you is far stronger than yours to him (v. 3). When we were unacceptable and at our worst, he bound himself to us with his covenantal love. Christ's marital fidelity to his bride is on full display at the cross, and it moves his bride to an increasingly sincere and pure devotion.*[1]

Here we see the same pattern as in the Old Testament: an unfaithful people and a faithful husband. Jesus the husband to the church is unfazed by our running around after other lovers. He has guaranteed his devotion and love to us eternally. His marriage promise to us was ratified on the cross of his suffering. And although he was actually married to us from eternity past, the day of his death was his presenting us with the engagement ring, the joining of ourselves to him. One day in the not-too-distant future we will have the wedding ceremony. The presenting of the bride to the groom will happen in heaven. In that place, the most epic of parties will take place. The couple will be united forever, never to be separated by sin, or fear, or distrust, or other loves. The love that the husband has always felt for the wife will finally be reciprocated in full. Jesus will be worshiped and loved the way he deserves.

The Beautiful Bride

The astounding part of the whole wedding imagery is how the Bible describes this unfaithful bride:

> Christ loved the church and gave himself up for her, that he might sanctify her, having cleansed her by the washing of water with the word, so that he might present the church to himself in splendor, without spot or wrinkle or any such thing, that she might be holy and without blemish.
>
> Ephesians 5:25–27

No spot, no wrinkle, washed completely clean, no blemish whatsoever. Every bride dreams of the day she is to be married and hopes that she can lose the right amount of weight, that she won't develop any blemishes the night before the wedding, that her hair will be just right, that her dress will fit her perfectly—all surface issues. You can sort of make do with what you have, but the deeper purity that is talked about in these verses is mind-blowing. Think about your life, think about your sin, and then hear these words: *cleansed, washed, splendid, blemish-free, holy, blameless.*

Spurgeon says of these verses: "The elect church is the favourite of heaven, the treasure of Christ, the crown of his head, the bracelet of his arm, the breastplate of his heart, the very centre and core of his love."[2] O Christian, do you think of yourself in these terms? Can you even fathom Jesus Christ thinking of you in these terms?

How Are We Made Clean?

When we, with solemnity, look at our lives, we see that we are anything but blameless. And yet, Christ calls us his *spotless* bride. How can this be? We can go back to Ephesians 5 for the answer. "Christ loved the church and gave himself up for her, that he might sanctify her, having cleansed her by the washing of water with the word" (vv. 25–26). I have heard this passage expounded on many times. I have heard preachers take it and make it all about how the husband should wash his wife in the Word or the Bible. The way for a woman to be clean is for her husband to read the Word to her. And while that is a good thing, it is not at all what this verse is saying. Women are not sanctified by what their husbands do or don't do. How hopeless would that be for a woman whose husband is not a believer? Men and women are sanctified by believing the gospel. We are made holy by what Jesus did for us, by how he has loved his church. We are made blameless by his giving of his life for us. We are spotless before him because our robes have been made "white in the blood of the Lamb" (Revelation 7:14). We aren't spotless because God looked down the annals of time and decided we would be a good fit for his kingdom. He didn't think, *Jessica will love me the way I deserve to be loved, so I am going to choose her*. No, instead he looked and saw my wicked, weak heart and said, "That is the one I will choose to love." "He saved us, not because of works done by us in righteousness, but according to his own mercy, by the washing of regeneration and renewal of the Holy Spirit" (Titus 3:5). The Holy Spirit reminds us of these truths, and as he does, we are washed and made clean.

The word that is talked about in these verses is the gospel. The gospel that proclaims salvation is his work alone. Salvation doesn't come to those who deserve it. The truth is, none of us deserve it. We could never work hard enough or be sorry enough to merit grace. He saved us because of "his own mercy" (Titus 3:5). This word of forgiveness and welcome makes us beautiful. We are made lovely by his love. He beholds us as a bride with no fault. Jesus' words to the church in these verses mirror those in the Song of Solomon: "You are altogether beautiful, my love; there is no flaw in you" (4:7). This is the word that makes beauty. Just as God spoke a word and creation was formed from nothingness, so the word of love spoken from Christ takes a dead person and makes him alive. In John 15:3 Jesus tells his disciples, "Already you are clean because of the word that I have spoken to you." This cleanliness is not some future state we have to achieve by our good words. It is a proclamation from Christ to you.

The gospel creates life, beauty, and the bride that we are. Imagine finding a gown from Vera Wang, a stunning, pristine white wedding dress. One that fits perfectly and makes you look so beautiful it is breathtaking to all those around, every curve perfect, every shimmer in the material bringing out the color of your eyes. It is as if the dress was specifically made for you. The cost of the gown is $25,000, which is totally outside of anything you could afford. But Vera herself hears about how you can't afford it and decides to give you the dress for free. You can't believe your luck! You gratefully accept the gown and then find the nearest field with the biggest mud puddle and immediately jump in the mud. That sounds like something a crazy person would do. And yet we stand in beautiful white robes and look around for ways to muddy ourselves. We look to other loves to find identity. We look to anything other than God for comfort and acceptance, and we try to rub dirt all over our dress. But the amazing thing is that the dirt doesn't stick. It can't stick. We can't change or alter God's final declaration of "faultless, beautiful, mine." Our wedding gown is washed once and for all because of Christ's finished work. Holy Spirit, give us faith to believe!

A Request

Before I start any discussion about how this applies to our marriages, I want to acknowledge that there may be men or women reading this who are in an extremely difficult marriage. You may be experiencing physical or verbal abuse or have an unfaithful spouse. If that is the case, I would encourage you to seek counsel and help from the elders of your local church. Please don't think that this chapter is going to be a cure-all for your marriage. You need help that reading a book can't give. You need people to walk through this with you. You may think, *If I can just love him or her better, they will stop their behavior.* I am pleading with you to tell someone what is going on.

There may be others reading this who aren't married yet. You may feel hopeless, as though you will never be married or remarried, or maybe you don't even want to get married. To you, dear brothers and sisters, I want to communicate that your marital status does not make you any less than those who are married. You are a valued member of the body of Christ. Press into the church; we need you.

And there may be still others who are married to unbelieving spouses. The pain that you carry every day is real and difficult. My hope is that you will find refreshment and peace in the truth that Christ is our heavenly Husband. I know there are days when that may help and days when you don't even care, but on both of those days, he looks at you adoringly and rejoices over you with singing (Zephaniah 3:17).

Marriage is not one-size-fits-all. Each marriage is unique as each person sins uniquely and has unique strengths.

Lastly, I want to confess that I am not a marriage pro. I don't have it all together. My husband and I fight. We go to bed angry at each other. We don't communicate perfectly, and sometimes we don't communicate at all. I am demanding and ungracious. He loves Jesus and for that I am grateful, because he has had plenty of reasons to leave me! We are both broken sinners in need of a Savior. It is only by the grace of God that we are still together.

I am not going to expound on the verses in Ephesians 5, 1 Peter 3, or Colossians 3. My guess is that you know those verses. If you don't, then go ahead and take the time to read them now. There are plenty of books out there that are excellent resources on our individual roles in marriage.

Know What to Expect

If there is a person you and I could single out in our lives as the one we sin against the most, chances are it's our spouse. We spend the most time with them and are the most emotionally invested in them. Their decisions affect our lives and vice versa. We have a power in each other's lives that is strong. I can be crushed by the way my husband, Cody, says "hi" to me when he gets home from work. And I can hurt him by my indifference toward him when he walks through the door. A lot of that is because my identity is tied up in how he loves me. If he is happy with me, then I feel like a beautiful bride. If he is angry or disappointed, or even if he has just had a hard day at work, I take that as his saying I am not good enough. That is my own deal, when I place the expectation on Cody to be my justifier, to be the one who declares, "You are loved. You are beautiful." In doing this, I am asking him to do what *only* Jesus can do for me. I am demanding that he fulfill the role of Savior in my life. I often think that if I can be a good enough wife and make him happy, then I will be okay. I find my okay-ness and my righteousness in how he feels toward me. This pressure is too much for anyone to bear. He can't be that for me. He will then feel my unmet expectations and withdraw, thinking he will never be enough for me. Which, in a sense is true—he can't be enough for me. I need my heavenly Husband's love.

Grace wins in this relationship too. When I remember that I am a sinner just like Cody is, I can extend the grace that has been extended to me. When I see that God loves me on my good days and on my bad days, I can love Cody without demanding he be the perfect husband. Beloved, when you and I remember that we are the unfaithful spouse to God, we can love our spouses when we don't think they give us the love we deserve. When I give permission to my husband to be human and to make mistakes, he in turn can love me when I am unlovable.

We place so many expectations on each other! Unrealistic expectations kill grace. Here is what you can expect: You married a sinner, so he or she will sin against you. Your spouse will be selfish and unkind, just like you are. Your spouse will be uninterested in your day, and weary with the sorrows of their own day, just like you are. Your spouse will need more than you can give, and that's okay. You can point them to Jesus instead of trying to justify yourself and act like you fulfill all their needs but they don't appreciate all you do. Stop trying to rub mud on your dress by expecting your spouse to be what only Jesus is.

Tullian Tchvidjian addresses the topic of expectations in his book *One Way Love*:

> We demand that our spouses perform and provide for us—or our spouses demand that of us. "You must save me. I need you to fulfill my unmet needs, because I can't." We use one another in the basest and most selfish ways: for our own self-aggrandizement. *One resounding principle here is that expectation is the mother of resentment.*[3]

What a glorious change would occur in our marriages if we truly believed that Jesus' love was all we needed and that that very love has been secured from eternity past.

Giving Up Our "Rights"

Most of the strife in a marriage occurs when we think we aren't being treated the way we deserve. This, of course, reveals an incredibly diluted and high view of how amazing we are. Tchvidjian has more wise words on this:

> A marriage founded on one-way love [grace] eschews scorekeeping at all costs. It is not a fifty-fifty proposition, where I scratch your back and then you scratch mine. A grace-centered marriage is one in which both partners give 100 percent of themselves. They give up their right to talk about rights. This means that a grace-centered marriage, in theory, is one where both parties

are constantly apologizing to each other, asking for and granting forgiveness. No one is ever innocent in a grace-centered marriage. If original sin is as evenly distributed as the Bible claims it is, then even in the most extreme and wounding circumstances, both parties have some culpability.[4]

I find it incredibly difficult to ask for forgiveness when the sin I have committed isn't a big one. Let me give you an example. When I am slightly cold to my husband or disinterested in his day and I can see that it hurts him, I just shrug it off and try to remember to be a better wife in the future. When I scream at him and slam a door in his face (shocking, I know), I am more apt to ask for forgiveness because my sin is out there in the open for the world to see. I think I can manage the "little" sins that are inward and not huge outbursts. The truth is that these "little" or "inward" sins are the ones that slowly destroy relationships. Little hurts that pile up on each other eventually form Mount I-Can't-Do-This-Anymore. I would venture to say that most marriages that end in divorce are not necessarily from one huge event, but rather from a drifting apart after years and years of ignoring sins against each other. The culture of our marriages should be a constant asking of forgiveness, acknowledging that we aren't the partner we should be, and then in humble repentance turning to our Savior.

Our heavenly Husband longs to be gracious to us. He waits to be patient. He has already forgiven us for all of our whorings, as far as the east is from the west—that is how far he has removed our sin of adultery from us. And even though daily, maybe even hourly, we slip back into adultery, you and I look for other loves when we have the ultimate Love in front of us. His steadfast love for us is fixed in the heavens. His love doesn't change depending on what we have done or how we have loved him or our spouses. He has no unmet expectations of us. For in Christ, we are completely accepted and completely welcomed. As we swim in the refreshing pool of this freedom we can invite our spouses to join us. We can laugh and play and remember that the health of our marriages is in his loving hands. Those same hands that were spread out on the cross for the forgiveness of our sins are the hands that take us and will ultimately bring us to himself.

8

Jesus Our Brother and Our Relationships With Our Families

*I*t is easy to forget that Jesus had a real human family. The only time we really think of his parents is when recounting the story of his birth or remembering Mary's grief when he was dying on the cross. We rarely give thought to the fact that he lived the majority of his life like you and me—with brothers, sisters, and a mother. We learn that sometime before his crucifixion his father died, and Jesus assumed the responsibility of the care of his mother, as observed when he gave his mother over to John while dying on Golgotha's hill (John 19:26–27). We've come to think of the fact that he was a son and brother as ancillary. It is, however, a very important and oft neglected truth that is beautifully comforting to us.

That Jesus had a family changes everything for us. Part of his humanity, part of the incarnation, was that he would experience all the temptations and trials that we go through. Regardless of the type of family life you have experienced, he can relate. He learned to understand the pain of a broken family. He suffered when sinned against by his brothers, sisters, and parents. He knows what it feels like to be harshly punished or lied about by a sibling because they are avoiding trouble. He knows what it is to be misunderstood by his family.

There's a story told in the Gospels that gives us a glimpse into the relationship he had with his family:

> While he was still speaking to the people, behold, his mother and his brothers stood outside, asking to speak to him. But he replied to the man who told him, "Who is my mother, and who are my brothers?" And stretching out his hand toward his disciples, he said, "Here are my mother and my brothers! For whoever does the will of my Father in heaven is my brother and sister and mother."

> Matthew 12:46–50

This may seem at first glance to be primarily a story about how we should obey the Father, but I think that if we look a little deeper, we'll find so much more happening here.

I have heard a lot of different theories on why Jesus' mother and brothers came to talk to him. Some say they were worried about his physical health. He had been traveling and teaching nonstop and perhaps they were concerned that he was fatigued or tired and needed to be told to take a break. Others think they were worried about his mental state, and to me this sounds the most viable. By this point in Christ's ministry it was getting around that he was making some pretty bold claims. In the same chapter of Matthew just a few verses before this story, the Pharisees are accusing Jesus of actually being of the devil. If the religious leaders of your time and in your city ascribed the work of Satan to *your son*, that would probably get back to you.

But what is so interesting to me is that Mary knew the truth about Jesus. She had been visited in a dream by the angel Gabriel, who said to her,

> Do not be afraid, Mary, for you have found favor with God. And behold, you will conceive in your womb and bear a son, and you shall call his name Jesus. He will be great and will be called the Son of the Most High. And the Lord God will give to him the throne of his father David, and he will reign over the house of Jacob forever, and of his kingdom there will be no end.
>
> Luke 1:30–33

She had become pregnant with Jesus without ever having had sex with a man. She heard the account of the shepherds, who came immediately after his birth to worship him because angels had told them to. When Jesus' parents presented him at the temple in accordance with the customs of the Israelites, Simeon and Anna both were filled with the Holy Spirit and confirmed to Mary and Joseph that Jesus was the Son of God, the Messiah. The Bible even says, "But Mary treasured up all these things, pondering them in her heart" (Luke 2:19). If there was anybody who knew who Jesus was, it was his mother, and here she was forgetting or doubting. That must have been so painful for Jesus.

We see exactly what his family thought of him in Mark 3:21: "And when his family heard it, they went out to seize him, for they were saying, 'He is out of his mind.'" This came after Jesus had healed a man's hand on the Sabbath. I am sure it wasn't just that he had healed on the Sabbath, but the way he had done it that upset them:

> And he said to the man with the withered hand, "Come here." And he said to them, "Is it lawful on the Sabbath to do good or

to do harm, to save life or to kill?" But they were silent. And he looked around at them with anger, grieved at their hardness of heart, and said to the man, "Stretch out your hand."

Mark 3:3–5

They must have been greatly confused. Here is Jesus, the one who always followed the rules, the one who was always kind, the one who always helped, the one who loved the Scriptures like no one they had ever seen before, and now this is how he is acting? He was surrounded by crowds of people who were fanatical about him. They wanted to see Jesus so badly that they pressed in on him to the point that he couldn't even eat.

The scribes and Pharisees were accusing Jesus of blasphemy against the Holy Spirit, saying he was of the devil, and his poor mother started to doubt what she had known so certainly at his birth. She must have already started to wonder. He was supposed to be something special, and yet he just stayed at home quietly working for thirty-three years. She probably had thought on more than one occasion, *Did I really see an angel? What did all that mean?* And then her son was performing miracles that were being ascribed to Satan's work, and she became devastated and tired and worried for him. No wonder she doubted.

And so we go back to the scene where Jesus has stopped teaching the Pharisees, who have dismissed him as a demon, and now he is teaching those who truly believe in him. It is to this location that his brothers and his mother rush in order to send a message through the crowds that they want to speak with him. It is too crowded for them to reach him, so up the message goes through all the different people there. Get the picture? It's not as though he's at a stopping point. He is in the middle of preaching and someone comes up to him and interrupts him with a message from his family. "Um, Jesus, sorry to bother you, but your family needs to talk to you right now." I can imagine that his mind flashed back to when he was in the synagogue at age twelve and his parents found and "corrected" him for being gone and he responded, "Didn't you know I had to be about my Father's business?" (See Luke 2:49.) No doubt here he is again thinking, *Why are they interrupting? I am about my Father's business.*

What the Jewish community would have expected him to do at that time would be to stop his teaching to go and see what his family needed. Family *absolutely* came before teaching. But Jesus, being the "norm-wrecker" that he was, said something that was astounding to those in attendance: "Here are my mother and my brothers! For whoever does the will of my Father in heaven is my brother and sister and mother" (Matthew 12:49–50). *Jesus wasn't disrespecting his family by these words; he was redefining family.* He was extending an invitation to all listening to become part of his family. This invitation was even for his own family, who were standing outside thinking they should take precedence. Jesus once again said that his primary loyalty was to his heavenly Father and his family.

At this point, I am sure his brothers were ashamed and embarrassed by him. *How dare he not stop and come talk to us?! Who does he think he is?!* Starting with the way he was born to now creating a stir everywhere he went, they probably had had enough. Jesus wasn't immune to it. He had to feel their displeasure. We see in the gospel of John that "not even his brothers believed in him" (7:5). And while this may seem hopeless—*If his brothers didn't believe, then who would?*—we find out that eventually at least a few of his brothers ended up being believers and his brother James wrote the book of James in the New Testament.

Another beautiful truth we see in this little story is that Jesus did not and does not play favorites. If there was ever anybody that should have been a shoo-in for his heavenly family, it should have been his earthly family, but he doesn't work that way. It is *never* about our family pedigree; it is *always* about his extravagant grace. That is great news for us; it means that our earthly family will never disqualify us from being brought into his family.

His Commitment to His Heavenly Father

When Jesus redefined family, he was saying that his heavenly family came first, forever. Maybe you have had to make that same decision. Your family at times doesn't understand your decision to be a Christian. They may think you are weak, delusional, or just plain stupid. Here is some good news for you if your beliefs have hurt your relationship with your family:

> Jesus said, "Truly, I say to you, there is no one who has left house or brothers or sisters or mother or father or children or lands, for my sake and for the gospel, who will not receive a hundredfold now in this time, houses and brothers and sisters and mothers and children and lands, with persecutions, and in the age to come eternal life."
>
> Mark 10:29–30

I love Christ's heart here. He doesn't say, *Suck it up! You will be fine! Don't worry about your family life!* No, instead he reminds us of what is going to come. He tells us about the happiness and the familial relationship that will outdo and undo the sadness and pain we experience now. Once we become part of God's family, we have brothers and sisters across the entire world all united by the Father's love for his children and the fact that our older brother, Jesus Christ himself, died in order to make us part of this family.

I Am Not Ashamed

I have an older brother and a younger brother. Like all good brothers, they sometimes do things that embarrass me, but I bet if you asked them, they would say I am the embarrassing one. I have learned to revel in our embarrassment together at this point in life, but I can remember times when my younger brother acted just like a younger brother does and I would get embarrassed. I would want to disown him as my brother and wish we didn't even know each other. If you have a younger brother, you undoubtedly know the feeling—that deep heart yearning for the earth to open up and swallow you whole.

Jesus never feels that way about us. Never. Not only did he secure our entrance into his family, he went a step further and proclaimed that "he is not ashamed to call [us] brothers" (Hebrews 2:11). How can this be?! How can Christ look at me and not be ashamed? Most days I do something that makes me ashamed of myself. If I am being honest, there are lots and lots of times I think he is ashamed of me too, so I hide from him. Instead of running to him in prayer, I look for ways to make myself comfortable, to ease my shame with food or drink or relationship.

The writer of Hebrews explains how Jesus can make his remarkable unashamed pronouncement that we are his brothers: "For he who sanctifies and those who are sanctified all have one source" (Hebrews 2:11). Sanctification is that slow, lifelong process of becoming more and more like Christ. And just in case there is any confusion, Jesus is the one who sanctifies, and you and I are the ones who are sanctified. Once again, in an act of incredible condescension, Jesus says we all have the same source; he is just like us. We are all humans. He shared our flesh, our bone, our blood, our body, and became human in order for us to know without a shadow of a doubt that he longs to identify with us. He refuses to view himself as better than us. Paul writes in Philippians 2:5–8,

> Have this mind among yourselves, which is yours in Christ Jesus, who, though he was in the form of God, did not count equality with God a thing to be grasped, but emptied himself, by taking the form of a servant, being born in the likeness of men. And being found in human form, he humbled himself by becoming obedient to the point of death, even death on a cross.

Our Big Brother

What images come to mind when you think about the words *big brother*? I know for me it is the stereotypical older boy hanging out on the playground watching out for his younger siblings. If he sees his younger sibling being messed with by someone, he strides over and takes care of business: *"You mess with my little brother, you mess with me."* Truly this is Jesus' attitude toward those who try to hurt his brothers and sisters (you and me!). He says that very thing in Matthew 25:40: "Truly, I say to you, as you did it to one of the least of these my brothers, you did it to me." It is a shame, because I think we have taken those verses and made them about us. We have made them about how we are going to love Jesus by loving others, and while that is part of what those verses are about, the main point is that Jesus is taking care of *us*. Jesus takes his brotherhood seriously. He owns that relationship in a powerful way. Unlike Cain of the Old Testament, Jesus' life shouts, "I *am* my brother's keeper!"

"A friend loves at all times, and a brother is born for adversity" (Proverbs 17:17). If there was ever a friend who loved at all times or a brother who was born to take part in our hardships, it was Christ. Jesus is the truest fulfillment of this verse. He doesn't shrink away from you and me when we suffer or mess up *yet again*. He enters into our suffering—loving, leading, carrying us.

All That He Has Is Ours

Part of being in a family is sharing each other's things. Or I guess I should say part of being in a family means we *should* share each other's things. I watch this at work in my own family. My two boys have shared a room from the beginning. Now they are fifteen and thirteen and this whole sharing thing is getting to be a bit too much for them. My older son, Wesley, would love his own space without having to deal with his younger brother. My younger son, Hayden, would also love his own room so he wouldn't have to be under big brother's watchful eye. Hayden has also lived his thirteen years getting all of Wesley's old clothes. By the time Hayden gets the hand-me-downs, they aren't new—they are tattered, and let's be honest, they are probably stained. This is so not fun, especially when Hayden has his own style and it is not the same as Wesley's.

This sharing with other people in our family can be difficult, but not so when we are permitted to share with Christ. This is a great deal for us when we think about Christ being our brother. Romans 8:17 tells us we are "fellow heirs with Christ." We have equal claim to all that is his. All the blessings, all the rewards he has earned are now ours. Even writing that out feels like I am stepping over a line. What has Christ earned for us? He has won for us relationship with Abba, Father. He has made it possible now and forever to be assured of our welcome into the Father's home. Every blessing he worked for is ours. And not only do we share in all of the riches of his righteousness, he shares . . . no, he *takes away* all the punishment for our badness.

What is Christ's is ours, no matter how we feel. Spurgeon puts it this way:

> You have come here weak and feeble, doubting, distrustful, and cast down, but I tell thee, weak though thou be, and in thine own judgment less than the least of all yet the same hand that wrote Christ heir of all things wrote thy name with his, and till a hand can be found that can blot out thy Redeemer's name thine shall stand and abide fair ever and ever.[1]

We cannot lose our inheritance and it cannot be taken from us, unless of course someone is strong enough to take Christ's inheritance from him. And just in case you think maybe, just maybe, someone can take Christ's inheritance from him, they'd have to go through Father God: "All are yours, and you are Christ's, and Christ is God's" (1 Corinthians 3:22–23). There is nothing that can separate us from this relationship, this one-way love that pursues us to the ends of the earth, woos our hearts, and then makes us his own eternally.

Our New Identity

Jesus' brotherhood gives you and me a new identity. J. I. Packer in his classic book *Knowing God* says,

> The immediate message of adoption to our hearts is surely this: Do I as a Christian understand myself? Do I know my own real identity? My own real destiny? I am a child of God. God is my Father, heaven is my home; every day is one day nearer. My Savior is my brother; every Christian is my brother too.[2]

Packer suggests we tell ourselves that truth every single day. On the days when you wake up overwhelmed by all you have to do, remind yourself that you are a child of God. On the days when you get to the end of the day and you can't believe all the sins you have committed, remind yourself that your Savior is your brother. On the days when you are sinned against continuously and trampled on by those around you, remind yourself that heaven is your home. On the days you think you just can't go on any longer, remind yourself that every day is one day nearer to being with him. On the days you feel alone and as if no one is there for you, remind yourself that you have a multitude of brothers and sisters in the family of Christ.

The Firstborn

"For those whom he foreknew he also predestined to be conformed to the image of his Son, in order that he might be the firstborn among many brothers" (Romans 8:29). Christ has loved and known us from eternity past, and has chosen us to be a part of his forever family. He is the firstborn of many brothers. The word *brother* in this verse isn't exclusive to males. Women are referred to as brothers and sons, and men are referred to as Christ's bride, so it all evens out! Jesus Christ is the firstborn brother in our huge family. He takes preeminence in everything, even in this. Because he is the firstborn, we are all being conformed to who he is, every day. Our big brother is the best, the first, the foremost of all the brothers. His perfect life and substitutionary death are the only reason we are even allowed into the family. I love this verse that talks about the first of many. If we ever feel like the kingdom isn't growing or that people aren't being saved, we can remember that Jesus Christ is the first of many. He promises to build his family, and he will have his way.

God knew us and brought us into his family before we had ever done anything good or bad. He foreknew and predestined us. He didn't foreknow us and predestine us to stay the same messed-up sinner we are; he foreknew us and predestined us to change slowly into the image of Christ. We become more like our older brother every day. This change may not look like what we would expect it to look like, it may not necessarily mean that we sin less today than we did yesterday, but it does mean that we are one day closer to being fully and forever changed: "Beloved, we are God's children now, and what we will be has not yet appeared; but we know that when he appears we shall be like him, because we shall see him as he is" (1 John 3:2). Imagine that day, when we see him, the One with nail-scarred hands and feet, the One whose heart has always been for us, the One we have always longed to see, our true and perfect older brother. We will see him and we will forever be changed. We will be done with all the pain and the sadness of now. The heartache of living as a broken son or daughter in a broken family will be a faint whisper of a memory that we thought we once had, and the truth of him and his love for us will be all-consuming.

My Family Here and Now

While that all sounds beautiful, a life free from pain, sadness, and tears seems so far away. How can the truth that my older brother is Jesus Christ change how I relate to my parents who are divorced? Can it really help me when yet another Father's Day is coming up and I don't even talk to my dad? Does Jesus being my brother change my relationship with my siblings who are always competing for everything even *now*? How in the world can it help with the fact that I always feel like a disappointment to my mother? Well, first off you can remember what I wrote about this earlier in the chapter: Your earthly family isn't all there is. There is so much more in store for you. All of the pain you have experienced at the hands of your family will be nothing compared to the glory and the hope and the happiness that are in store:

> For this light momentary affliction is preparing for us an eternal weight of glory beyond all comparison, as we look not to the things that are seen but to the things that are unseen. For the things that are seen are transient, but the things that are unseen are eternal.
>
> 2 Corinthians 4:17–18

Our family life is transient. It moves on. It is only a short period of time compared to what is true and lasting and eternal.

Forgiving our families, extending grace to those who have hurt us, is a difficult thing. As we remember that we don't deserve to be a part of Jesus' clan, it will help us to be able to love the unlovable. Christ had every right to ask us to prove that we want to be part of his family, to prove our love for him. Instead, he stunningly loved us at our worst. The very moment that you and I were enemies of his Father, the moment we hated him, that was the moment he awoke our hearts to his mercy and grace. We don't have to demand proper retribution. We are free to love those who have made terrible mistakes and those who have purposefully hurt us. This doesn't mean that you put yourself in a situation where you will be physically harmed, but it does mean that you can learn to let the gospel seep into those parts of your life that are the darkest. Sometimes we hide the hurts from our families and lock them away in the deepest parts of our hearts. We are afraid to let anybody see or even let ourselves experience the pain of our past because we don't know if we will recover from it. Hear this truth: Jesus has accepted us into his family. He has changed where we are from and who we are. He has promised that every pain will be redeemed, every terrible experience will find its hiding place in the wounds of Christ.

Expecting Christ From Sinners

A lot of the everyday sin we commit against each other in our families is because we are expecting them to love us perfectly, and they can't. I don't want to diminish the real hurt that we undergo as we live with and around other sinners, but I do want to make sure we have realistic expectations. We expect our parents never to sin against us, our brothers and sisters never to compete with us, our grandparents to always cherish us—expectations that are impossible for anybody to meet. If you want a realistic expectation, here it is: "All have sinned and fall short of the glory of God" (Romans 3:23). Expect to be sinned against. Expect your parents to hurt you and not always be there for you. They are fallen humans . . . just like you are. Expect your siblings to fight with you and disagree with you. They are also fallen humans . . . just like you are. Expect your grandparents to make decisions that are unwise at best and unkind or even cruel at worst. They are fallen humans . . . just like you are.

The majority of those in your family are not out to hurt you purposefully. The truth is that they are broken and don't know how to love the way they should. They are selfish and care more about their own problems than they do yours. They are busy trying to make it through their own days and don't often think of how to best help or care for you. This is true of all of us. When I think of all the ways I have failed my family, I can become depressed and wonder why I am such a screw-up. The truth of the gospel says, yes, you are a screw-up, but you are a loved screw-up who has a heavenly Father who cares for you, and a Big Brother who is looking out for you.

Our Past/Our Future

You may not have had a hard childhood. As a matter of fact, when you reflect on it, you think it was really good. A loving father and mother created a sense of security for you, you got along well with your siblings and didn't experience any long-standing conflict with them, and good memories fill your mind when you reminisce. But even the best of families is just a shadow of what God is like and of the love we receive from our Older Brother. People who grew up in healthy families often tend to idolize the family, making it an ultimate thing instead of appreciating it as simply a good thing. I know that is my experience. I had a great childhood, and even though my parents made mistakes, they loved each other and they loved Jesus. They sinned against us and against each other, but we always seemed to work it out. I am such a broken, messed-up person that I take even this good and warp it. I struggle against thinking family is the most important thing. The ultimate thing. While family is important, it is not the most important. The story of Jesus not going out to his family when they wanted him to evidences this.

When I make too much of my family and life isn't what I want it to be and things don't go how I want them to go, I get angry or scared. For instance, if I want to have a family day together and my husband ends up having to work, then I tend to get mad because there are emergencies in his line of work and he can get called away at any moment, or worried that he doesn't get to spend enough time with the kids. My anger and worry are true signs that I think my family is the most important thing and that I have to hold everything together all the time or it will fall apart. But when I relish in and rest in the truth that Jesus is my Brother and God is my Father, then I am able to spend time with my children without worrying. I can trust that even this silly inconvenience of my husband having to work instead of joining our family day will be used by God to draw my children closer to him. I don't have to be angry because I know that my Brother cares for and loves in an extravagant, life-giving way.

A good family life or a bad family life doesn't define you; it doesn't have to be your identity. You are free from that on either side of the spectrum. This is good news for you and me. You don't have to live up to the perfect standard you thought you were raised with, and you don't have to be enslaved to your past. Sammy Rhodes is a pastor, blogger, and hilarious tweeter, and he wrote an exceptional blog on this very subject. He talks about the pain of having a father who was addicted to crack cocaine, but how Sammy applies the gospel to this part of his life is breathtaking. He says,

> Passing down what you would never want to pass down. This is the irony of family. Tragedy might be the better word. Wounded people wound people. Often in ways completely un-intentional and entirely different from the ways they themselves were wounded. My grandfather wounded my father. My father wounded me. How will I wound my children?
>
> They say that hope is borrowing from the past and the future to invest and infuse the present with redemptive meaning. That our stories can have happy endings no matter the broken beginnings. That our lives can know incredible change from the inside out. That generational sin can be broken. Lord, I believe. Help my unbelief.[3]

Jesus is your brother; he loved you when you didn't deserve it. He cares when you forget about him. He lives every day to pray for you. He is always presenting you before God, reminding him that you are part of the family (Hebrews 7:25). You don't have to look to your past; you don't have to be defined by how you grew up. You can love the screwed-up family you were born into because Jesus brought you, a total screw-up, into his family. God's love for you isn't based on your performance as a son or a daughter or a brother or a sister. His love is based on the performance of his Son. He has done it all. Paul David Tripp puts it like this:

> The shattered relationship between Father, Son, and Holy Spirit at the cross provides the basis for our reconciliation. No other relationship ever suffered more than what Father, Son, and Holy Spirit endured when Jesus hung on the cross and cried, "My God, my God, why have you forsaken me?" (Matthew 27:46). Jesus was willing to be the rejected Son so that our families would know reconciliation. Jesus was willing to become the forsaken friend so that we could have loving friendships. Jesus was willing to be the rejected Lord so that we could live in loving submission to one another. Jesus was willing to be the forsaken brother so that we could have godly relationships. Jesus was willing to be the crucified King so that our communities would experience peace.[4]

You are free to forgive and free to ask for forgiveness. You are free to stop expecting everyone to be for you what only he can be and is for you. You are free to look to your Older Brother to take care of you. He will. Forever.

9

Jesus Our High Priest and Our Relationships With Church Members

here are 19,000 churches split or scarred by major conflict each year. That means that 50 churches are significantly impacted every day due to serious conflict.[1] Pastors sin against members of their congregation. Members of the church sin against their elders. Friends in small groups sin against each other. The list goes on and on. The words "Of all people, he should know better," and "I thought we could expect more from the pastor and his wife," and "I shared so much of myself with that group of people; why would they turn on me?" ring out in every single church in America.

Why are so many people disillusioned by the church? Why is it that "1,500 pastors leave their assignments every month in the United States because of conflict, burnout, or moral failure"[2]? You have probably either been significantly hurt by someone in the church or watched a friend go through a terrible rending of relationship. Why do the wounds from the church sting so much?

Even as I am writing this I know of several churches that are imploding. I know of elders bringing charges against other elders, emails sent in haste and anger, words spoken aloud that can never be unheard, and friends gossiping about other friends. We are truly a collection of broken people with jagged edges cutting other broken people around us. Social media doesn't make the problem any better; it actually expands it beyond our individual communities and pushes it into the world. Almost any day of the week you can find an article decrying a celebrity pastor or a large organization on Twitter or Facebook. If you want to find someone who is unhappy with their church, all you have to do is Google the name of the pastor and most of the time an angry blog will come up.

What Is the Church?

In the *New City Catechism* the church is defined like this:

> God chooses and preserves for himself a community elected for eternal life and united by faith, who love, follow, learn from, and worship God together. God sends out this community to proclaim the gospel and prefigure Christ's kingdom by the quality of their life together and their love for one another.[3]

The Bible describes the church in 1 Peter 2:9–10:

> But you are a chosen race, a royal priesthood, a holy nation, a people for his own possession, that you may proclaim the excellencies of him who called you out of darkness into his marvelous light. Once you were not a people, but now you are

God's people; once you had not received mercy, but now you have received mercy.

I have often heard it said that church is not somewhere you go, but rather it is who we are. We are the church.

When I look at those descriptions of the church, there seems to be a huge discrepancy in what I see as a reality and what I know we should be. It can oftentimes be discouraging when I see the gap. One of my favorite Christian rap artists, Lecrae, takes those two realities of what we are and what we should be and talks about them in his song "The Bride." He says, "Yeah she may look gritty, When her man come back she gone look so pretty." He goes on to describe this discrepancy with lyrical genius. The bottom line is that we are not yet what we are supposed to be, but one day we will be.

Who Is in Charge of This Mess?

Honestly, who would want to own that mess? I look at the church and I think, *Really? Who takes responsibility for this?* Just as we saw in the previous chapter when God our husband owns a prostitute of a wife, Jesus calls this church his own. He claims ownership of the church and says that he is our High Priest, he is the leader, and he is responsible (Hebrews 2:17).

The high priest is not a concept we encounter in modern-day culture. In order to understand it, we must take a little time for a history lesson. Now, before your eyes glaze over and you go into skim mode, please take the time to read and understand this concept. I promise you it will be jaw-dropping, gratitude-creating, awesome. You will no longer think of a long robe with bells on the bottom. Instead, when you hear the words *High Priest*, you will see Jesus and be grateful that he has taken this role upon himself.

145

A High What?

In Exodus 28, we see the implementation of the role of the high priest. *The Gospel Transformation Bible* notes,

> Although God's people had heard God's voice (20:19–21), and although they were to be a "kingdom of priests" (19:6), God established a priesthood to mediate between himself and his people (28:1–2). He chose Aaron and his sons "from among the people of Israel" to serve in this way, identified with their fellow human beings as representatives and in weakness (Heb. 5:1–4).[4]

The high priest was a role that one could only obtain by birthright. He had to be in the lineage of the Levites. He was held to a high standard of behavior and purity. The high priest would share the priestly roles of the other priests, with one exception. Once a year on the Day of Atonement, he would enter the Holy of Holies. Again from *The Gospel Transformation Bible* we read,

> God dressed Aaron in "holy garments" that would serve to cover his sinfulness and make him fit to stand in God's presence (Ex. 28:4). These garments shared the same kind of fabrics as the tabernacle, showing that the priest's ministry was a heavenly one.[5]

The high priest would get decked out in his high priestly robe and enter the temple. Once inside the temple, he would take off his high priestly garments and only wear his under linen. Then he entered the Holy of Holies and sprinkled blood on the mercy seat. This act would make expiation, which means it would purify the people from their sin and guilt. He would make atonement for the Israelites. Atonement is the act of making God and man one: "at-one-ment." Everything that was in the way of a relationship between holy God and sinful man was done away with by the expiation of our sins and the procurement of our forgiveness.

Now, if you don't see Jesus in that act, I don't know what to say! He was taken to the cross wearing a mock priestly robe of purple, stripped down to his underlinens, and made to bleed. When he died, the curtain that separated the Holy of Holies from the common temple was torn. The removal of the separation invites us into the Holy of Holies, making a way for us to be clean enough. Christ was better than the high priests of the Old Testament because he made a perfect sacrifice once for all.

The high priest was a representative for the people. The one who could make them clean before God. The one who offered up sacrifices for their sins. To us this is hard to understand. We are not amazed by a high priest because we have never had to rely on another person to help us attain the forgiveness we need. But to the Hebrews who saw the high priest slaughter animals daily—the shedding of blood to atone for their sins—this thought was revolutionary. With the proclamation of Jesus as their High Priest, they no longer had to have another human ask for their forgiveness; they no longer had to bring an animal for it to be sacrificed. They were given permission to go straight to God because of the perfect sacrifice that his Son made. They were given direct access to their heavenly Father and they were assured that their sins were paid for. The sacrifice had been made and had been accepted by God. This, in and of itself, was shocking.

Not Just Forgiveness, But Understanding As Well

Forgiveness of sins and being in relationship with God is amazing news, but that is not all Jesus does for us in his role as our High Priest. Hebrews 4:15–16 says,

> For we do not have a high priest who is unable to sympathize with our weaknesses, but one who in every respect has been

tempted as we are, yet without sin. Let us then with confidence draw near to the throne of grace, that we may receive mercy and find grace to help in time of need.

He sympathizes with our weaknesses. You see, if he didn't sympathize with us in our weakness, how could we come boldly before the throne of grace? We wouldn't be able to; we would forever be hiding in the shadows, always wondering if he was angry with us. I fear that is how many Christians live their lives—hiding, wondering—and he is telling them to come boldly, assured of his mercy and grace. How overwhelmingly kind is he?

This last week, I was in Alabama from Sunday through Tuesday, home on Wednesday and Thursday, and then I left again for Colorado on Friday and Saturday. Saturday was my birthday, and I spent it speaking and flying. I came home, and on Sunday and Monday I was discouraged. I was angry. After I travel and speak, I often experience a deep and unmovable sadness. I know some of it is physical exhaustion. The back and forth between time zones takes a toll. I also know some of it is a spiritual attack.

Even admitting that it is hard to travel and speak makes me feel vulnerable. Maybe you will think something like, *Oh, it must be hard to get to travel and talk about Jesus. And have everyone treat you like you are something special.* I get it—it sounds a little silly to talk about what I get to do as being hard. But at the same time, I really do struggle. I love what I do and I see it as a privilege and an honor, but I still struggle. You see what I felt like I had to do there? I had to explain myself, make sure that you see it from my point of view, make sure you see all of my heart in this. Here is what is so cool about Jesus: He sees me, knows that I have a hard time, knows my weakness, and he doesn't judge me. He doesn't judge me for even one second. He only sympathizes with me. In my unbelief and my anger this last week, he was praying for me and loving me.

I would venture to say that there are areas in your own life where the fact that he sympathizes with you would be of real comfort. When you are struggling and feeling condemned by your sin, have you ever stopped and thought, *Even in this he doesn't condemn me?* Maybe if we start praying that the Holy Spirit would remind us of this truth, we would find the allurement of sin lessen in our lives. Scotty Smith says, "Our sins do not separate us from the love of Jesus; Jesus separates us from the love of our sin, and from sin's guilt and power."[6]

Gentle With the Ignorant and Wayward

The entire book of Hebrews is an argument convincing us that Jesus is better. Better than the old covenant, better than the high priest that the people at the time were accustomed to, better than all they had known to that point. Jesus was, however, in some ways the same as the high priest they were used to: "For every high priest chosen from among men is appointed to act on behalf of men in relation to God, to offer gifts and sacrifices for sins. He can deal gently with the ignorant and wayward, since he himself is beset with weakness" (Hebrews 5:1–2). Jesus was chosen from among men and appointed by God, just like the high priests of old. Jesus offered sacrifices for sin, just like the high priests of old. Jesus deals gently with the ignorant and wayward, because he himself was beset with weakness. He was fully human. He understood what it was like to have a human body, human emotions, human hormones, and he understood weakness.

The incarnation brings unceasing hope and an end to our exile, wandering, and despair. There is great comfort for our souls

149

in the truth that he is just like us. Here's why: the incarnation tells us that even though we sin, we are not alone; even though we're weak and finite, he knows what weakness and mortality are because he was weak and mortal just like us; and even though we continually fail, he has committed himself to be part of a race of failures—and he has done so forever. He does not use our flesh merely as an impersonal dwelling place, like some seedy motel room he can't wait to vacate; rather, he assumes our nature completely and will be the God-man forever, throughout eternity!"[7]

Christ binding himself to us as a human, as our High Priest, means that he gets us in a way that no one else ever has or ever will. O Beloved, this is such amazing news. It helps me when I feel like I can't go on anymore because one more failure would undo me. It proves to me that he isn't peering down his nose at me, disgusted with my humanness. This truth gives me courage when I am lonely and feeling isolated, or when I am hiding because I am ashamed at my own sin. He isn't angry at us and it doesn't stop there; he deals gently with us as we struggle. What kindness is this? He is perfectly gentle with the wayward (those who purposely sin) and the ignorant (those who just don't know any better).

Tempted As We Are

Not only is Christ called gentle "with the ignorant and wayward," Hebrews goes on to describe him in this way: "For we do not have a high priest who is unable to sympathize with our weaknesses, but one who in every respect has been tempted as we are, yet without sin" (Hebrews 4:15). He was tempted as we are—what a glorious thought—and yet was without sin—even more glorious still. John Piper preached a sermon in which he talked about what it means for Christ to be tempted:

> And he can sympathize with us in our allurements to sin, because he was tempted—
>
> - to lie (to save his life)
> - and to steal (to help his poor mother when his father died)
> - and to covet (all the nice things that Zacchaeus owned)
> - and to dishonor his parents (when they were more strict than others)
> - and to take revenge (when he was wrongly accused)
> - and to lust (when Mary wiped his feet with her hair)
> - and to pout with self-pity (when his disciples fell asleep in his last hour of trial)
> - and to murmur at God (when John the Baptist died at the whim of a dancing girl)
> - and to gloat over his accusers (when they couldn't answer his questions)
>
> Jesus knows the battle. He fought it all the way to the end. And he defeated the monster every time. So he was tested like we are and the Bible says he is a sympathetic High Priest. He does not roll his eyes at your pain or cluck his tongue at your struggle with sin.[8]

We are almost afraid to ascribe this type of humanity to Christ, but it is in the Scriptures. How can he be tempted in every way, unless he was really tempted in every way? The Creator of the Universe, the all-powerful I AM, was made like us so that he could better relate to us. The One who holds all things together by the word of his mouth, the one in whom the fullness of God dwells, was made a man in order to understand your struggle with sin and my struggle with sin. If that wasn't enough, he walked on the earth and he endured being weak and endured being tempted, and he did it perfectly. This gives him the right to then say, "See?! It can be done! Just obey! Just resist temptation like me!" But this isn't his demeanor toward us. No, he then is sympathetic with us. He paid for our constant succumbing to sin with his death on the cross. Is his patience never-ending? He never sinned, and yet he never gets weary with our sin. His sacrifice was perfect and perfectly accepted.

Spurgeon puts it this way: "There is never an exceeding heaviness, nor a sore amazement, nor a wound of treachery, nor a stab of ingratitude of which He did not feel. The sharpest arrows in the quiver of anguish have been shot at his dear heart."[9] Why? Why did he have to feel such pain? It is for you and me, so that we can believe without a shadow of doubt that he is for us. Octavius Winslow echoes Spurgeon with this:

> He is not a High Priest who can be indifferent to your present assault, since He was pierced by Satan, and in a measure is still pierced by the fiery darts which now pierce you. *Accept your present temptation as sent to make you better acquainted with His preciousness, His sympathy, His grace, His changeless love.*"[10]

Even though Christ is in heaven, he still feels for you.

I've heard that this word *sympathizing* is akin to this picture: If you put two pianos in the same room and you strike a note, putting hammer to string, on one of the pianos, the same string on the other piano will vibrate. That is a picture of Christ's heart and our own. If one of his family is hurting, his heart hurts in the same way.

Always Making Intercession for Us

Not only does Christ deal gently with us, and sympathize with us in our temptations, he lives to make intercession for us! It just keeps getting better. Hebrews 7:25 says, "Consequently, he is able to save to the uttermost those who draw near to God through him, since he always lives to make intercession for them." Do you ever feel alone? Like no one cares or sees? He cares! He sees! He prays for you.

I often tell my friends that I will pray for them and I forget or I get too busy, but not our Savior. I can remember one time specifically when a friend told me they were going to a doctor's appointment to find out if a cyst was cancerous or not. I had promised to pray. I had even put it into my calendar to remind myself to pray at the time of the appointment. I wanted my friend to know God's peace and love so desperately during such an uncertain time. Of course when the time of the appointment came I had left my phone in the other room with the volume off. I heard from my friend the next day. She told me how she knew I had been praying because she felt so much grace during the appointment. My heart sank. I hadn't prayed; I hadn't even remembered the appointment. And when I got the text from her the next day, it even took me a couple seconds to process what the heck she was talking about. But the beautiful thing is Jesus himself was praying for her. He was loving her, being a perfect High Priest, living to intercede for her.

He is never too busy to pray. He is always busy praying. "But, day without night is our Intercessor pleading. He never intermits; His love never cools; His ardor never decays."[11] He prays passionately for you with deep interest and love. There is no end to his role as High Priest. "The former priests were many in number, because they were prevented by death from continuing in office, but he holds his priesthood permanently, because he continues forever" (Hebrews 7:23–24). He will forever be praying for us. From our first breath until our last, he is breathing out prayers of intercession for us. There is absolutely no time, no circumstance, no sorrow, no happiness, where he is not thinking about us and presenting us before the Father.

What Is He Praying?

We can observe how Jesus prayed for his people in two different instances. First, we can see how he prayed for Peter. Before the crucifixion, Jesus reveals to Peter that Satan wants at Peter. Jesus tells Peter that "I have prayed for you that your faith may not fail. And when you have turned again, strengthen your brothers" (Luke 22:32). Then Jesus goes on to tell Peter that he will deny Jesus three times before the rooster crows. It is interesting to me that he doesn't ever tell Peter not to deny him. What he does is reassure Peter that after he does deny him, Peter's faith will not fail because Jesus has prayed for him. Jesus then tells Peter that he can go ahead and strengthen his brothers after his crazy failure. Jesus is praying for you and me right now, and he is offering up the same prayer . . . that our faith won't fail. I am pretty sure that all of his prayers are answered with a "yes" from the Father.

Second, we can see how Jesus prayed for us in the High Priestly Prayer of John 17. Jesus is praying to his Father immediately before going to the garden and then to the cross; he is pouring his heart out before the Father. He is praying for himself, for what he knows is about to happen is going to be excruciating for him and for his disciples. What else does he pray? He prays that God would "sanctify them in the truth; your word is truth" (v. 17). It is astonishing that the Word made flesh is praying that we would be sanctified by him, the truth about the entire story of redemption. This story was about to reach its climax in the coming days of Jesus' life, with his gruesome death, burial, and glorious resurrection. This prayer was about to be fulfilled in the act on the cross. The cross and resurrection is the answer to the prayer.

What Truth Sanctifies Us?

Hear the other petitions that Jesus pours out before the Father in this prayer, the truths that Jesus pleads for us to know:

- God sent Jesus.
- Jesus came to glorify God by doing the work of redemption that God sent him to do.
- The church was a gift from God to Jesus!
- Once we are his, we will always be his.
- We are eternally kept by the Father.
- We are guarded by Jesus.
- Before the world ever existed we were loved by God.
- We have an irrevocable and eternal union with Christ.
- God loves us as he loves his perfect Son.
- Fullness of joy comes from knowing God's love for us in Christ.
- Just as God and Jesus are one, we are one with Christ.
- Jesus longs for us to be with him.

Loved As Jesus Is Loved

Three times in the last four verses of John 17 our eyes are opened to the powerful, evocative love the Father has for his Son and for us:

- "that the world may know that you sent me and loved them even as you loved me" (v. 23)

155

- "you loved me before the foundation of the world" (v. 24)
- "that the love with which you have loved me may be in them, and I in them" (v. 26)

How my heart longs for and simultaneously militates against believing that God loves me as he loves Christ. I want to believe that I am loved so perfectly, so greatly, but I know my failings and I know I don't deserve such love. Even in knowing my unworthiness, I try to prove myself, by my own good works, and the truth I need is found in these verses. I was loved before I ever did anything good or bad. As Sinclair Ferguson says, "Our status is not a matter of our worthiness, but of His love."[12]

The truth of belovedness is what sanctifies. The truth of the wonderful story of redemption is what sanctifies. It is too good for our legalistic hearts to believe and yet it is the truth that sets us free from our legalism. In your struggle against sin, in your struggle to be a more "sanctified Christian," remember the truth of God's love for you in Christ. It changes everything. Our sanctification is completely about him and his work in our lives, his completed work, his ongoing work.

About this, Octavius Winslow wrote,

> Oh, how precious is this truth in the consciousness of our many failures and defects! Our salvation is all in Christ—our righteousness is all in Christ—our merit is all in Christ—our completeness is all in Christ—in Christ our Covenant Head, our Surety and Mediator; and no flaw in our obedience, no defect in our love, no failure in our service, should so cast us down as to shut our eye to our acceptance in the Beloved. . . . We are fully and eternally complete in Jesus.[13]

He is praying now and forever that our faith won't fail and that we will be sanctified by the truth of his love.

Spurgeon wrote,

> If our Lord was thus sympathetic, let us be tender to our fellow men. Let us not restrain our tender feelings, but encourage them. Love is the brightest of the Graces of God and most sweetly adorns the Gospel. Love to the sorrowing, the suffering, the needy, is a charming flower which grows in the garden of a renewed heart. Cultivate it! Make your love practical! Love the poor not in word only, but in actual gifts to them! Love the sick and help them to a cure![14]

As we see how he has stooped so low in loving us, we can surely love those in our church communities. We can bear with one another's weaknesses, being patient because he has been so kind and patient with us.

Bearing With Each Other's Weaknesses

As I have said in every other chapter, judgment and unmet expectations kill relationships. And let's be honest, judgment runs rampant in the church. We expect so much from each other. After all, we are all Christians. The unspoken motto of the church is "Be better, do better," and when we see other members of our community fail, we have a difficult time being honest about their failures. We hate seeing how utterly depraved we all really are. Not only do we have a hard time facing our own brokenness, we despise when it forces its way to the surface in others. We try to numb the pain of sin by disdainfully treating others with a "come on, you know better" attitude. If we allow their brokenness to show, then we will be confronted with our own brokenness, and we cannot bear that. We like to keep the church looking pretty. We feel that if the church can't look nice, then what is the point?

I fear that we err significantly by expecting the church to be pretty. Ironically, if there were ever a group of people that should be able to bear with someone else's weakness, it should be the church. In our very going to the Sunday gathering and being part of a church, we are admitting that we need help, that we aren't perfect. And yet, so many put on their best masks on Sunday morning. We hide our weaknesses and brokenness because we want to measure up to the other "super Christians" in the church. You can probably recall a time when you decided to take the mask off and be honest and then were immediately "taught good theology" and told to "trust God." The pain of the reprimand confirmed to you that it was a bad idea to ever remove the mask. In that moment, you may have resolved not to be open with those in the church, because they just don't understand. In walking around trying to fix each other, we have lost the art of accepting each other, brokenness and all. Instead of fixing each other's broken parts, what if we started bearing with each other's broken parts? I am not calling on the community of believers to never point out sin, but I am asking us to see and mimic how Jesus has been with us.

The Great Masquerade

Paul Miller, in his wonderful book *A Loving Life,* talks about how to walk with people who are suffering. In the book, he goes through the life of Ruth. He says,

> What can we say to Naomi's lament? Nothing. Absolutely nothing. We just weep with her. That is good theology, to weep with those that weep. God does not lecture Naomi. Nor should we lecture those who are grieving. It is a striking example of Jesus's command to "judge not" (Matt. 7:1).[15]

When is the last time you just sat with a friend in your church and cried with them without trying to make everything all better? We can trust God with the hearts of our fellow church members. After all, he was the one who brought them into the kingdom to begin with; we can have confidence that he will help them along the road of sanctification. We don't trust the Holy Spirit to do his work with our friends.

And, if we're honest, we don't trust the Holy Spirit to do his work in us either. We are scared to be who we truly are because we are afraid if we are honest about the depth of our depravity, no one will love us. This fear and secrecy is the default setting of our hearts. Adam and Eve's first thought after sinning was to hide and cover themselves. The only thing that obliterates this hiding is the gospel. The truth is that we are more sinful and flawed than we ever let ourselves believe, and we are more loved and welcomed than we ever let ourselves hope.[16] That thought will change all of our relationships. Why would we be shocked at the sin of another church member? They are sinful and flawed just like we are. We are free to love sinners because that is who Jesus loves.

It is true we need to have sorrow over our sin and not take pride in the way we hurt others, but we are also called to look realistically at who we are. We can own our brokenness without trying to cover it up with all of the other parts of us that aren't as broken. For instance, if I am bad at caring for people, I make myself feel better by reminding myself that I am a good housekeeper. I am sure everyone reading this has certain areas of goodness that they prop themselves up with when they see how they fail. Just like Adam and Eve, we frantically run around trying to hide our nakedness with the fig leaves of our "goodness." Next time you are confronted with something that you have done wrong, see where your mind wanders. Do you justify

159

it? Do you try to remind yourself that you really aren't that bad a person? We think we can cover our badness with our goodness, and Christ is calling us to be rid of both and to look to him for all of our comfort and acceptance. We don't have to prove ourselves to ourselves or to others anymore.

You and I are similar to the Pharisee in the parable in Luke 18:9–14. We think that if we can just be better than the next guy, we will be okay. We look at those who are public with their struggle and we say, "Thank God I am not like them." In other words, "Please put your mask back on; your brokenness is showing." We hide our sin instead of being like the tax collector who pleads the mercy of God on his life, the one who doesn't care if his brokenness shows, because he is sick of trying to hide it. The truth of the matter is, both the Pharisee and the tax collector are equally broken, but the Pharisee tries to hide his brokenness with his good deeds: "I fast twice a week; I give tithes of all that I get" (Luke 18:12).

Sisters and brothers, can we stop acting like the cross wasn't for us? Can we take off the masks? You are loved. You are free to be honest about who you really are. You are free to let others be honest about who they really are. God is big enough to handle it all. He really is.

In Him We Are One

So how do we do this? How are we honest about our struggles and our failures? How do we love those who are struggling and failing? We can remember that we are all joined together in Christ, and in him we are one.

> Walk in a manner worthy of the calling to which you have been called, with all humility and gentleness, with patience, bearing

with one another in love, eager to maintain the unity of the Spirit in the bond of peace. There is one body and one Spirit—just as you were called to the one hope that belongs to your call—one Lord, one faith, one baptism, one God and Father of all, who is over all and through all and in all. But grace was given to each one of us according to the measure of Christ's gift.

Ephesians 4:1–7

We remember that we are all in this together. We have the same Father, and he has been so gracious to us. We remember that grace has been given to each of us in different measures. That may mean that someone in your church body struggles with the same thing over and over and over. It means that God is allowing that person to sit in their sin, and we can love them right where they are. The Holy Spirit is strong enough to make a dead heart alive to God. He is certainly strong enough to make us stop sinning altogether if he thought that was best for us.

So we are humble with one another, not thinking we are better than others. We are gentle with each other, instead of beating each other over the head with a long list of "you-shoulds." We can point out sin, when necessary, without distancing ourselves or acting like our friends have a disease that we might catch if they don't get their acts together. We bear with one another in love, which is tough, especially if their sin affects us personally. And we are eager and excited to maintain peace, instead of eager and excited when we get a juicy bit of gossip about our friend. We remember that we are one body, and if I hurt you, I am actually hurting myself. We take a vested interest in each other and in loving one another. Lastly, we remember that all of our failures to live as one body have been paid for by our Savior. We don't have to hide from our community when we sin against them. We confess and remember that even the sin of hurting others in the church was paid for on Christ's cross. We pray for a new and deeper understanding of what he went through to make us one body, and we pray that this understanding changes who we are as individuals and as a community of believers, one redeemed sinner at a time.

10

Jesus a Carpenter and Our Relationships With Our Co-Workers

*H*ave you ever spent time thinking about what Jesus' life was like before he started his ministry? Have you considered that he spent time doing chores to help Mary around the house? What was it like for him to live with his family? How did he feel as he learned how to work in Joseph's workshop? How do you go from humble carpenter to one who is able to perform miracles? In the book of Mark, we have a very brief glimpse into what he did before he started his ministry. Apparently it was the first time he had returned home since setting out to start proclaiming the good news:

He went away from there and came to his hometown, and his disciples followed him. And on the Sabbath he began to teach in the synagogue, and many who heard him were astonished, saying, "Where did this man get these things? What is the wisdom given to him? How are such mighty works done by his hands? Is not this the carpenter, the son of Mary . . . ?"

Mark 6:1–3

Those Jesus had grown up around couldn't believe what they were seeing and hearing. Here was Jesus, the boy who came from a questionable beginning as evidenced by their slander of him as the "son of Mary." This description wasn't just a way to talk about who his parents were. The people were specifically referring to the fact that Joseph wasn't his dad. The second aspect of their mocking is the reference to him as a "carpenter." They're incredulous that he could be anybody important when his life to that point had been spent as a "carpenter."

Joseph was a carpenter and had taught Jesus his trade. This was traditional in that time period. A father was responsible for teaching his son to carry on his work. In Matthew 13:55, Jesus is referred to as a "carpenter's son." Imagine with me for a moment, Jesus and Joseph in their workshop. Jesus' hands clumsily using the tools, accidentally hitting his own hand with the hammer. Joseph gently taking those hands and saying, "Try it one more time, son." Jesus knew the heartache and the frustration of not being able to create what you are trying to create.

There was no going to college to learn or deciding what you should do with your life. If you were a male, you would just do what your father did. That was your career path. Jesus was no different. He took up Joseph's trade and worked as a carpenter until he was thirty. Generally speaking, it's easy for you and me to gloss over these years of his life and not even think about the significance and comfort those years should bring to our work and work relationships. Elyse Fitzpatrick puts it beautifully in her excellent book *Found in Him:*

Jesus willingly hid himself away in Nazareth for thirty years. Generally ignored, he toiled without complaint, suffering humbly on our behalf. He lived as Jesus the child, big brother, carpenter, and single man providing for his family. He voluntarily adopted all these roles for us. His life as a young man with sawdust in his eyes, serving his widowed mother and siblings, was no meaningless placeholder while he counted the days until he could step onto the scene to do something really important. No, he wasn't merely treading water: He was living life for us, and he was being perfected through the suffering of life in a sin-cursed world. It was for us that he suffered, lived, and loved every day for thirty years. The one who didn't grasp after the equality with God that was rightfully his, "emptied himself" and became a servant (Phil. 2:6–7) and learned by experience what it was to be "gentle and lowly in heart" (Matt. 11:29) as he suffered in human frailty year after year.[1]

Every day of his life was spent fighting to love. He fought to love and obey while working as a carpenter. He worked hard to provide for his mother and siblings. He understood what it was like to have customers who weren't pleased with the work. Because people are the same as they were back in the days of Jesus, I know that there were customers who tried to cheat him. I know that he had to deal with people who changed their minds mid-project. You can rest assured that anything you have to deal with as one in the workforce, Jesus had to deal with also.

Our Workplace

Jesus' being a carpenter should bring great comfort to those of you who do manual labor. The Son of God did manual labor; there is nothing demeaning about it. God does not consider you "less than" if you don't have a job that is "full-time ministry."

Among Christians, there's often an undue significance placed on working in a church or for a nonprofit organization. It is almost as if your work doesn't matter as much if you are just a banker versus being a counselor for the church. Jesus Christ himself was in the "secular" workforce for most of his life. There is no shame in that; there is no "less than" in that. His work assures us that a sales clerk is just as important as a pastor. Now, before I go any further, I am not saying that pastors or counselors or missionaries are not important. They are absolutely important. We need them for the growth and well-being of the church, but they are not more important than those who are in the secular workforce every day.

> A. W. Tozer, writing in *The Pursuit of God*, clarifies that "one of the greatest hindrances to internal peace which the Christian encounters is the common habit of dividing our lives into two areas, the sacred and the secular . . . so that we live a divided instead of a unified life." This false dichotomy between sacred and secular has become entrenched in an institutional way in the church. A "calling" to so-called "full-time Christian ministry" (missions, pastoring, teaching at a seminary) is often perceived as having greater value to God than those roles without this "calling" (e.g., business owner, plumber, homemaker). Sadly, such hierarchical valuing negatively impacts believers in business.[2]

Martin Luther fought for this very truth during the Reformation. The church at that time placed a special importance on those who had given their lives to work in the church. The priests were treated as royalty, they received special gifts, and their word was thought infallible. Luther wanted everyone to see the importance of their own particular vocation or calling. He recognized that each one of us is called and gifted differently. He talked about how every vocation, each job, is actually God's work. God is empowering every human being with productive employment to help others. Luther says,

> All our work in the field, in the garden, in the city, in the home, in struggle, in government—to what does it all amount before God except child's play, by means of which God is pleased to give his gifts in the field, at home, and everywhere? These are the masks of our Lord God, behind which he wants to be hidden and to do all things.[3]

What a beautiful concept that in our work "we are all the hidden masks of God." The woman who helps you at the fast-food counter, the man who takes your mail, the person who gathers the carts in the parking lot at your local grocery store are all God working. God pours out his mercy on the just and the unjust. He uses the just and the unjust to help and serve their neighbors. This should inform and change the way you and I treat all of these people. They are all made in the image of God and doing the work of God, and we should give them the dignity due to them. Would anybody dare say that Jesus' work was "less than" because he was a carpenter? My guess is no. So why do we treat people who do work for us with contempt or impatience? We are forgetting how Christ himself elevated the role of one who works with his hands. We are also forgetting that they are created in the image of God, and as image-bearers they deserve our respect.

Jesus the Servant

> Christ Jesus, who, though he was in the form of God, did not count equality with God a thing to be grasped, but emptied himself, by taking the form of a servant, being born in the likeness of

men. And being found in human form, he humbled himself by becoming obedient to the point of death, even death on a cross.

Philippians 2:5–8

Christ wasn't just a carpenter who went home at night thinking his work was done. In the very act of the incarnation, Christ took unto himself the title of *servant*. That word *servant* is the same word used to describe slaves in Ephesians 6.

What condescension, for the Son of God to come and place on his own shoulders the yoke of slave to all. The word *servant* means he was placing himself in subjection to others. He was fulfilling the great commandment to love God and love others. "The Son of Man came not to be served but to serve, and to give his life as a ransom for many" (Matthew 20:28). His whole life and his death were meant to point to the fact that he didn't come to make much of himself. He didn't come to get his proper due. He didn't come to be treated right. He came to serve and to give. Here he is, once again, not just telling you and me that we should serve each other, but *showing* us how to serve and how to love. And truly, the beauty of this is that now it is our record. He not only died for all the times we serve ourselves instead of others, but before God we have his perfect record of a life of complete service. "For you know the grace of our Lord Jesus Christ, that though he was rich, yet for your sake he became poor, so that you by his poverty might become rich" (2 Corinthians 8:9). This is his heart toward you. He gives all so that we can have the best. He binds himself to us with his eternal bands of love.

In the Old Testament, there was a provision given to an indentured servant who had finished the time he owed his master if he wanted to stay with the master. By law he had to serve six years, but if at the end of the six years he loved his life with his master, this was the provision:

But if the slave plainly says, "I love my master, my wife, and my children; I will not go out free," then his master shall bring him to God, and he shall bring him to the door or the doorpost. And his master shall bore his ear through with an awl, and he shall be his slave forever.

Exodus 21:5–6

What a beautiful picture of what Christ has done with us. He was pierced for our transgressions. He made a covenant to be ours forever. He even now still serves us by interceding day and night before the throne of his Father (Hebrews 7:25).

Jesus is not a servant whom we can command to do our bidding and expect it to be done. But he has *chosen* to lay his life down for us in the most humiliating way. He does work everything for our good and for his glory. He loves to work for us and through us. How invincible is this love? Does it know no limits?

American Dream/Nightmare

Take a minute to think about the guiding principle of American culture—"do what makes you happy" and "find what you are passionate about and pursue that." While there is nothing wrong with doing what you enjoy or looking for a job that you are passionate about, we have made a terrible point of our focus. We are setting out to fulfill *ourselves* instead of looking for ways to serve *others*. How often do we really think of our jobs as a way to be God's hands, even if our job is just stacking books at the library? God's great commandment to love him with everything and love our neighbor as we already love ourselves can be fulfilled every day as we get up to the sound of our alarm clock. Even for stay-at-home moms who don't have a paying job in the workforce, the vocation or calling to be a mom is just as important as the vocation or calling to work outside the home. No matter what you do, you are called to serve and love others the way you have been served and loved.

This self-focus has caused much distress in the workforce and in the home. When a man goes to work and hates his job because he doesn't see any value in it, doesn't feel like he is getting paid what he is due, doesn't like the way he is treated, and thinks that in general he is getting the short end of the stick, this will affect his vocation as father and husband at home. When we start to believe our jobs are about *us*, and not about loving God and loving others, then we will experience pain and discontentment. That is not to say that we should just stay in a terrible job with an awful employer, but we should continue as long as we think it wise and go to work every day focusing on loving and serving.

The American Dream has actually turned into a slavish night-mare. The harder we try to be well-respected and fulfilled in our various callings in life, the more brokenhearted we will become. It is never enough. You will always have someone "higher than" you in the company, or if you are the boss, there will always be another boss who is making more money and seems to have a more successful business. I am not just talking about those who work outside the home. This is just as true in all of our vocations: as a spouse, a daughter, a mother, and an employee.

Think about the contrast of Christ to the American Dream, willingly choosing to become the least, a servant to all. He didn't just do it for people who loved him. It is easy for me to be a mom and serve my kids when they are really grateful and kind. But when they talk back or are unappreciative, I don't want to do anything for them. Most of the time I tell them, "Fine, if you don't like the dinner I cook, you can do it tomorrow." Or as an employee, "If you don't like the way I do that job, why don't *you* just do it?"

Jesus wrecks this karma-principled way of working by serving those who were his enemies, serving the ones who don't deserve to be served. His work wasn't dependent on the one who received the benefit of his work. His work was only and always dependent on his love for God and his love for people.

What Do You Do?

When you meet somebody you don't know for the first time, what is one of the first questions you typically ask them? I know for me an easy way to learn about someone is to ask, "What do you do for a living?" While this is a valid question, it is not only how we learn about people but also how we tend to judge them based on their answer. If someone says, "I am a brain surgeon," we automatically think: *rich and smart*. If someone says, "I am a janitor," we may make judgments that aren't so kind. If someone confesses that they don't have a job at the present time, we often uncharitably think they are lazy. If someone tells us they own their own business, we may think them to be resourceful or ambitious. Even though we have a suspicion that judging people by what they do is wrong, we do it anyway. And we know that we are judged by what *we* do. This just feeds into the fact that we find our identity in our vocation. We find our value in how much we get paid. We give ourselves over to the opinions of our fellow employees. We find comfort and joy when our boss is happy with our work. We are devastated or angry when we have customers who don't appreciate the hard work we have put in for them.

We submit ourselves to the slavery of finding our identity in our work, and we demand that everyone else find their identity in work also. When they don't play the corporate game, we think something is wrong with them. Before all of us stay-at-home moms feel better about ourselves in comparison to those judgmental corporate types, remember that we do the same thing. When we find out that a mom works and puts her kids in daycare, we feel a slight air of superiority because we have made the decision to be home with our kids. This judgment of each other happens across the board: with how we educate our children (homeschool vs. public vs. private) to how we feed our children (organic vs. processed) to how much time we let our children spend with media (one hour vs. play as long as you like just as long as you don't bother me). If you're a mom who works, you may feel as if you are pulling your weight in a way that women who don't work outside the home don't understand. We all take pride in how hard we work. We are trying to earn our own approval or others' approval or even God's approval. We wear our "hard days" like a badge of honor, making sure everybody knows all the adversity we had to endure that day. Again, let's be sure that we know the driving factor: We are looking for validation in our work. We are looking to prove that we can earn our keep, that we are worth something, that we have value and meaning. The problem is that the very thing we are looking for in our own work performance, we already have in Jesus' performance and in his work.

Let me give you an example of how I find my identity in my work in a small, seemingly silly way. As an author, I receive free books from other authors. The hope of these authors is that I will use my influence to promote their book. I love books, I love reading, and I also love getting anything for free. So when I receive one of these books in the mail, I feel validated. I feel like I must have a lot of influence and my word is good as gold and that is why the author thought to send the book to me. I walk away from the mailbox with a spring in my step, head held high. Now, on the flip side, when I don't receive any free books for weeks or months, I start to wonder if I am worth anything. I have fleeting questions about whether I will really ever make it as a Christian author, if my voice is worth anything, or if my opinion is to be trusted. Now, I understand how silly that looks. There could be a myriad of reasons why I haven't received any books, and yet I jump to crazy conclusions. I would ask you to stop and consider whether there is an area in your life that is tied to your vocation where you do the same thing.

I know I also do this in my vocation as a mother. When my children are loving and laughing and wanting to be around me, I feel like I am the best mom ever. When I get compliments on how smart or how kind or even how athletic my children are, I swell with pride and am convinced their goodness has to do with all the hard work I have put into raising them. Conversely, when my children are quiet or withdrawn or angry or disobedient and when I have to hear from other parents about something my kids have done wrong, I get sad or angry. I start to feel like all of my hard work is for naught and wonder why God even made me a parent.

What is the answer to this? How can I stop finding my identity in my vocation, or in my performance in my vocation?

First of all, let me relieve you of the pressure of thinking you will ever get to a place where you don't find some identity in vocation. Because we are sinful and we never really believe Jesus is enough, you and I will struggle with this for our entire earthly lives. There will come a day, though, when we are free from it. We will see him and be changed in a moment, in the twinkling of an eye. All thoughts of ourselves will be forever banished and we will be utterly consumed with him.

Second, the answer to how we strive against this slavery of identity in vocation is to fight to find our identity in him. Pray that the Holy Spirit shows you that what he has done for you is the most important thing about who you are. Once you are freed from trying to prove your worth, you will be free to love and serve others and to love God.

Who Do You Really Work For?

In Ephesians 6:5–8, Paul shares practical help for employees:

> Bondservants, obey your earthly masters with fear and trembling, with a sincere heart, as you would Christ, not by the way of eye-service, as people-pleasers, but as bondservants of Christ, doing the will of God from the heart, rendering service with a good will as to the Lord and not to man, knowing that whatever good anyone does, this he will receive back from the Lord, whether he is a bondservant or is free.

I love how gritty these verses are. They just blow through the pretense and strip us of all the reasons we normally try to be a good employee and then give us a better motivation. We aren't to be good employees because we want to gain approval. If this is true of us, we'll be tempted to only work hard when we are in front of others, or when our boss is watching, and these verses tell us that is not a good thing to do. I absolutely love the reason given that this is not a good thing to do: Paul is saying to us, "Why would you just seek the acceptance or approval of your employer? You aren't really even working for them. You are working for Christ." Once we get a hold of that, it changes everything. It changes how we work, because we no longer just try to get the bare minimum done. We are working for Jesus. It changes how we treat our boss, because we know that even he or she has an ultimate authority, and it allows us to submit to our bosses without fear of what they will do to us.

The verses also talk about working "from the heart." This means that the gospel changes your motives for why you work. At one time you would work only for self-gratification or to make money, but because Jesus has worked for *you*, worked to make you his own, now you work with a changed heart. You work because you love God and you love others. And then again, Paul reminds us that we are working for God. It is almost like Paul can read our worrying minds here: *Well, if I don't do my work for my employer, if I don't work extra hard when he is around, then how is he going to reward me for my efforts?* The Holy Spirit speaks through Paul and gently tells us that we don't have to worry about that either: "We will receive from the Lord what we have worked for." This changes our relationship with our employer because we aren't always expecting from them. We aren't working to be noticed; we aren't working to be acknowledged. If this is true, we won't be consumed and constantly taking the temperature of our employer's attitude toward us. We also won't have to steal glory from our fellow employees. When they do something good, we can congratulate them without fretting over the fact that they did something better than us. We don't have to use others in our companies to achieve our end goal of being well thought of; we can look for ways to help others look good too. Why? Because he sees, he knows, and ultimately, he rewards.

Who's the Boss?

In our passage in Ephesians, Paul doesn't just talk to the employees, he also has some instruction for the boss: "Masters, do the same to them, and stop your threatening, knowing that he who is both their Master and yours is in heaven, and that there is no partiality with him" (v. 9). In a shocking turn of events, Paul gives the same advice to the masters as he does to the slaves! I am sure we have no idea how shocking this command actually was. In those days, the master had complete control over the life of the slave. He could legally beat or imprison or sell his slave if he didn't perform well enough. And here comes Paul by divine inspiration of the Holy Spirit, and he just flips it. He levels the ground by giving the same commands to both. "Do the same to them." He tells them to let their attitude toward their slaves be ruled and motivated by their relationship to their own master in heaven. If you are a boss, remember that you are a servant of God and treat your employees accordingly. You are not the ultimate authority; there is someone who has authority over you. How does the gospel of grace change the way you act as a boss? You stop threatening your employees; you don't manipulate or abuse them. I love how Paul in essence is saying, "Remember that God doesn't care about your position of authority over them. It doesn't matter to him. He doesn't play favorites based on position." How gracious is our Master! He gives the same precious truth to both employees and employers; it is truly God who is in charge. This relieves the pressure from the boss to keep everything together. He can trust and rest in God.

Entrust Your Soul

If you are a boss or an employee, if you are a stay-at-home mom, or a working mom, or a student, the answer to all of your vocational relationships is to "let those who suffer according to God's will entrust their souls to a faithful Creator while doing good" (1 Peter 4:19).

Fulfill your vocation, but don't count on it to fulfill you. Trust your soul to your faithful Creator. He is truly the God who sees.

He is your ultimate Master; you work for him. You are valued by him no matter what your calling is. He loves you with an everlasting, invincible love. He will take care of your every need. And in all the ways you fail at your vocation, he forgives you. In all the ways you push to get to the forefront instead of becoming a servant and looking out for the interests of others, he forgives you and loves you and continues to serve you. You don't have to fight to be the best. You can believe that he gifts each of us uniquely, and while you may not be the best at what you do, you can be faithful and grateful for the opportunities to serve in your position. You can help others pursue their vocations, encouraging them and helping them. All the while remembering how you have been served and loved by Jesus and how your true Master is faithfully loving you.

11

The Holy Spirit Our Comforter/Helper and Our Relationships With Difficult People

s there someone in your life who makes you cringe? Perhaps if you see them in the grocery store or walking toward you after church, you pray for the earth to open up and swallow you. I am sure you can think of a few people in your life who are hard to love. It may be as simple as their personality just grating on you. I have a pretty laid-back personality, and when I am around people who are type A, I have a hard time. Whenever I am around them, I find myself thinking: *I just don't understand why everything is so important.* In the reverse, I am sure they are looking at me and asking, *Isn't anything important to you?!* Our personalities don't mesh. I know intellectually that I can learn from them and should probably take things a bit more seriously, but that doesn't change the fact that I want to roll my eyes at everything they say or that they are probably wishing I would just get my act together!

Even more complicated than dealing with conflicting personalities are the times you and I encounter people who can just be mean. They don't care about what you think, say unkind things in an unkind way, and hurt you continually. This may be because their lives are a mess and they are living out of hurt, or it may be because you have offended them in some way and no matter what you do, you can't seem to make things right. And it may also be because they choose to be mean to others. It is just who they are.

Regardless of the reason for their attitude toward you, I am sure you could easily list a few people in your life right now that you wish would disappear. You don't want them dead or anything awful like that; you just want them to move away and never contact you again.

You could probably also think of others in your life who have caused you tremendous pain and grief. People who have broken you, people whose sin against you has scarred you. People who took from you something you will never get back. People you have hated in your heart. I don't want to make light of the pain that others have caused in your life or pretend there is any easy fix. I have often read that if there is a person in your life who has hurt you, you should just think good thoughts about them and all will be better, or just make sure you pray for them daily, or do nice things for them, and while all of those things are good advice, they don't ever get to your heart and they completely leave the Holy Spirit's work out of the equation.

Finally, think about the people in your life whose lives are marked by constant, severe suffering. It seems as though week after week of painful circumstances pile on, turning into months and then years. We all have friends whose lives are just more difficult than what seems normal. These friends need you to walk with them and help bear their burden. While you love them and count it a joy to walk with them, you experience and feel their pain in real ways. You feel helpless and at times hopeless that anything is ever going to be better for them, and yet you know you must be strong for them.

Francis Chan calls the Holy Spirit the *Forgotten God*, and in his book by the same name he says,

> From my perspective, the Holy Spirit is tragically neglected and, for all practical purposes, forgotten. While no evangelical would deny His existence, I'm willing to bet there are millions of churchgoers across America who cannot confidently say they have experienced His presence or action in their lives over the past year. And many of them do not believe they can. [1]

I fear that most advice on how to deal with difficult people leaves out the most important help that is available to us. There are two aspects of the Holy Spirit that are invaluable keys to loving the unlovable or loving those in hard circumstances.

This chapter is not meant to be an in-depth study of the Holy Spirit, but rather a framework for you to understand his role in relationships a little bit better.

Someone Better

In John 13, at the Last Supper, Jesus is talking with the disciples and is explaining to them what is about to happen. He realizes that his time with them is coming to a close: "Jesus knew that his hour had come to depart out of this world to the Father, having loved his own who were in the world, he loved them to the end"

(v. 1). Stop, look, and reflect on the verse one more time. He loved them who were his own and he would love them to the end. It is so beautiful that he continues loving even to this day. Part of loving his own was knowing that when he left, they would be discouraged and dismayed. So he is trying to give them hope in these last few hours together, telling them that what is about to happen isn't the end. He gives a couple promises for them to keep fixed on when everything else gives way. He is teaching them why it is good for him to go.

First, he says he is going to prepare a place for them. He tells them he longs for them to be with him, but in order for that to happen eternally, he must leave. Then second, he tells them that once he goes, the Holy Spirit will come:

> And I will ask the Father, and he will give you another Helper, to be with you forever, even the Spirit of truth, whom the world cannot receive, because it neither sees him nor knows him. You know him, for he dwells with you and will be in you.
>
> John 14:16–17

He tells them that, better than having him stay with them, the Holy Spirit will be sent: "Nevertheless, I tell you the truth: it is to your advantage that I go away, for if I do not go away, the Helper will not come to you. But if I go, I will send him to you" (John 16:7). If anybody knows what is best for you and me, it is our Savior, and he says it is better for us if he leaves and the Holy Spirit comes. It was for our *joy* that the Holy Spirit was sent to us. But in order for that to happen, Jesus had to die and be raised on the third day and then ascend to heaven. So for the next few pages, let's remember who the Holy Spirit is and the significance of his being sent to us. I am counting on the fact that as you remember, you will see how you need him desperately in all of your relationships—from the most difficult to the easiest.

Our Helper

"But the Helper, the Holy Spirit . . ." (John 14:26)

"And I will ask the Father, and he will give you another Helper" (John 14:16)

"But when the Helper comes . . ." (John 15:26)

"If I do not go away, the Helper will not come to you." (John 16:7)

In each of these verses, the Holy Spirit is described as our *Helper*. That word in the Greek means, "one who helps, by consoling, encouraging, or mediating on behalf of—'Helper, Encourager, Mediator.'"[2] It also carries the meaning of "one who is summoned to the side of another" to help him in a court of justice by defending him, "one who is summoned to plead a cause."[3] Get this picture in your head: the Holy Spirit is the one you want on your side in the courtroom of life, right next to you. His job is to remind you of how beautiful Jesus is. His job is to reassure you that you can call God "Abba, Father." He opens our eyes to see that we actually aren't standing in a courtroom waiting to be judged, but rather sitting in the Father's living room relaxing on the couch. He is constantly singing in your spiritual ear songs of how much you are loved. I once heard Tullian Tchividjian pray that the Holy Spirit would come and convince us that the gospel is true. That is his work. The Holy Spirit guarantees the gospel is true. He works in our hearts as a promise of this truth (2 Corinthians 1:22). He is a spotlight that shines on the loveliness of Christ. He is committed to the spread of the gospel. *The Westminster Confession of Faith* says,

He prepares the way for it [the gospel], accompanies it with his persuasive power, and urges its message upon the reason and conscience of men, so that they who reject its merciful offer are not only without excuse, but are also guilty of resisting the Holy Spirit.[4]

This is his work in the life of believers and in the life of those who don't believe. His job doesn't stop once you make a profession of faith; it continues as he carries on reminding you every day that the gospel is for you.

That's not all he does, though. He is also your advocate before God the Father. He is there to pray for you. Romans 8:26–27 says,

Likewise the Spirit helps us in our weakness. For we do not know what to pray for as we ought, but the Spirit himself intercedes for us with groanings too deep for words. And he who searches hearts knows what is the mind of the Spirit, because the Spirit intercedes for the saints according to the will of God.

So not only is he speaking to you, he is speaking to God on your behalf. Praying for you. Presenting your case before God. Praying perfectly because he perfectly understands God's will. Once again, I love that Paul tells us that the Holy Spirit knows our weakness. He knows that we don't know how to approach God and so He does it for us. The Holy Spirit was himself the one who first opened your eyes to believe the gospel, and he will continue to do so. We need reconvincing every day. We need to hear that we are forgiven and loved and that the gospel really is all we need.

Let's look to *The Westminster Confession* one more time for clarity on who he is and what he does. Take time to read this and pray that the Holy Spirit will apply it to your heart:

The Holy Spirit, whom the Father is ever willing to give to all who ask him, is the only efficient agent in the application of redemption. He regenerates men by his grace, convicts them of sin, moves them to repentance, and persuades and enables them to embrace Jesus Christ by faith. He unites all believers to Christ, dwells in them as their Comforter and Sanctifier, gives to them the spirit of Adoption and Prayer, and performs all those gracious offices by which they are sanctified and sealed unto the day of redemption.[5]

God is ever willing to give him to you, to be your comforter and sanctifier. He is there to help you believe that your adoption is irrevocable. He is there to help you see how your adoption will help you to pray. You don't have to worry about having a good day or a bad day; you are in the family and have full access to the Father. That is what the Holy Spirit is there to remind you of. On those days where you feel a cloud of displeasure and feel like you can't pray, ask the Holy Spirit to remind you of who your Father is and why he has decided to make you a part of his family.

My Comforter and Those Who Are Uncomfortable

The only thing that will help you love and continue in relationship with people who are unlovable is the Holy Spirit. His ever-soothing voice reminding you of Christ's love will calm your heart. I know that when I am around a person I find difficult, all I want to do is hide. I want to look for an escape. I don't want to be hurt yet again. I go into defensive mode and try to build a wall of protection. The walls I build are typically made of sarcasm or distance. If I have to be around *that* person, then I will just be sarcastic with them and try to avoid letting them into any place in my heart that might cause pain. I also like to use distance. Sure, I will be there in person but I will be distracted, or at least I will act distracted. I can even go so far as to try to hurt them before they hurt me. A slight jab of unkindness here and an annoyed look there, and maybe they will just back off. You see, I know better. I know I am not to be like that, but I also know I can't change my own heart. I would have done it by now. I hate this sin in my heart. I pray that God changes me. I am desperate for his work in my life.

I know of others who deal with difficult people by trying their hardest to appease their every wish. They tiptoe through the minefield of pleasing them and hope that they don't step on anything that will blow their foot off. Even though it may look like they are loving that difficult person, being kind and working to make the person happy, they are actually completely fearful and hating the person in their heart. The more they try to please, the more they hate them, because they see that the person is never pleased. Have you ever noticed how when you find out that someone you sort of like doesn't like you back, you try even harder to get them to like you? You are simultaneously angry at them and trying to win their favor at the same time. The more they push you away, the more you want them to approve of you. This never-ending cycle is destructive and reveals the idolatry of others' opinions. Difficult people rip away our fig leaf of good reputation and it hurts. We like to think we are likable, and when someone doesn't like us or doesn't treat us the way we want to be treated, we realize that maybe we aren't all that great. This thought destroys us, and so we look for ways to make it less hurtful. We tell ourselves that *they* are actually the awful person. We convince ourselves that they just misunderstand us. We protect ourselves and steel our hearts.

The difficulty is heightened when these are people whom we are committed to love—they are in our lives and are not going anywhere. Maybe you have a wayward child who has made it his life's purpose to harm you and run from you. Maybe you never got the love and protection from your parents that you needed. Maybe you have a person in your small group who always knows exactly what to say to set you on edge. Maybe a dear friend betrayed your confidence and has sought reconciliation, but you find trusting her difficult. There are many different scenarios that include the necessity of continuing a relationship with a person who is unlovable. Let me, however, make this very clear: If you are in relationship with someone who is causing you physical pain and injury, you are not ever called to stay in that situation where you could be harmed. We are not called to stay in a physically abusive relationship, ever. There are most assuredly different levels to this conversation. I understand that.

When you are in relationship with difficult people, the only hope you have of continuing to love them and not giving up in despair or going into hiding is the comfort that the Holy Spirit can bring you. Even in the most trying and difficult of circumstances, he can help you persevere. Abraham Kuyper puts it this way:

> For the Holy Spirit does not dwell in our hearts as we dwell in our house, independent of it, walking through it, shortly to leave it; but He so inheres in and cleaves to us that, tho we were thrown into the hottest crucible, He and we could not be separated. The fiercest fire could not dissolve the union. Even the body is called the temple of the Holy Spirit; and tho at death He may leave it at least in part, to bring it again in greater glory in the resurrection, yet as far as our inward man is concerned, He never departs from us. In that sense He abides with us forever.[6]

Jesus didn't describe the Holy Spirit as comforting, but as a person who is the Comforter. That is what he will be to you in times when you feel like you just can't let your heart be hurt one more time. He comes to you when you can't even imagine there is any hope left and when you feel as though there will only ever be pain. He comes and envelops you in his presence. He teaches you love by loving you. In those moments where your pain is wholly yours, he is wholly yours as well. He lifts your burden and gives you glimpses into the beauty of the Trinitarian love for you. Assured of this love, you can then love. You can give. You can persevere.

Through the Holy Spirit, you and I can love when we've been hurt. We lay down our preference for a certain type of person because the Holy Spirit loves unity. It is his very presence that makes unity in the family of God possible. I realize that the person who is difficult in your life may not be a Christian. If that is the case, you can start praying right now for their salvation and redemption. In 1 Corinthians 12, we see more of the heart of the Holy Spirit: "For in one Spirit we were all baptized into one body—Jews or Greeks, slaves or free—and all were made to drink of one Spirit" (v. 13). We are part of him, we drink of him, and so we are a part of each other. No one is better than anybody else. Let me say that again: You and I are not better than the person with whom we struggle. That is painful to write, and I honestly want to backspace. I have deluded myself into thinking I am better, but the truth is, I'm just not. I am just as dependent on the Holy Spirit as anybody else. I need him just as desperately.

Our Counselor and Friends in Hard Places

Like me, you may have dear friends who suffer terribly. I know of people who just seem to have lives that are marked for suffering. It seems as soon as one trial passes, another one is waiting at the doorstep ready to seize them by the throat. It almost seems unfair that they would have to go through so much. I find doubt creeping into my own heart, and I am sure it has a hold of theirs as well. I doubt that God has their situation in control. I doubt his love for them. I mean, why would he let them experience so much suffering? While you deeply love these friends, it can be hard to continue to walk next to them, especially when you feel you don't have the fix they desperately need.

Part of the reason I struggle to be around people who suffer is because I have to come to grips with my own inability to make everything better. I hate to see that I am actually not the Holy Spirit and I can't bring them the comfort they need. I hate that I say the wrong things at times and I end up hurting more than helping. But I believe it is in embracing that very weakness that the Holy Spirit has more room to work. The more I try to make it better, the more I try to come up with the perfect verse, the more I am ultimately in the way. When I relinquish the desire to be the Savior and just grieve with my friends, the Holy Spirit does some pretty amazing work.

I am not saying we shouldn't share encouraging Bible verses or try to help our friends with good resources, but I am saying we should leave room for just being still with them. The stillness of grieving is so hard for us. We are like the Galatians, who forgot who started the work in their lives. We think it's now our job to keep our friend's head above water, to keep them holding on. Thankfully, it is never your job to do that; it is the Holy Spirit's work alone. Paul's words to the Galatians have meaning for us in the times when we think what we do will save someone from their misery: "Let me ask you only this: Did you receive the Spirit by works of the law or by hearing with faith? Are you so foolish? Having begun by the Spirit, are you now being perfected by the flesh?" (3:2–3). You and I aren't perfected by the work we do, and we can't perfect others by the work we do either. We are perfected by the Holy Spirit; he is the only one who changes hearts.

Sounds a bit silly and obvious to say, but he is better at being a counselor and a comforter than we could ever hope to be. Of course we know that, but do we functionally live that? Part of the frustration and hopelessness we feel when we can't help others or don't say the right thing is because we think we are going to be the one who gives them just the right advice that will change their entire lives. Unlike us, the Holy Spirit never tires in his efforts to comfort God's children. He never fails in his timing. He can move a heart in ways that we can't even imagine. He never gives the wrong advice. He never speaks too harshly. He is what our friends need. He is what we need. When we feel at a loss and incapable of helping, in that moment, we can cry out to the Holy Spirit to do the work he lives to do. In our admitted weakness, he proves himself so strong.

The Holy Spirit may use you to speak words of comfort and wise counsel. I know there are times when I have been in situations when I just felt him work. He used me to say words I never would have come up with on my own, and he has used other people to speak truth and encouragement into my life that I desperately needed to hear. All through the book of Acts we see times and places where the apostles were filled with the Holy Spirit and able to speak to the people in ways that opened hearts. In Matthew 10:19–20, Jesus spoke directly to his worried disciples. He knew they were concerned that they wouldn't know what to say or how to share the good news of the gospel with others. Jesus responded to their anxiety, "Do not be anxious how you are to speak or what you are to say, for what you are to say will be given to you in that hour. For it is not you who speak, but the Spirit of your Father speaking through you."

The Holy Spirit speaking through you.

What if we took the time to really pray before we answered someone? What if we took the time to actually listen to everything they said without formulating some plan of attack to solve all of their problems? What if we actually trusted the Holy Spirit to speak through us? I understand this won't always work out perfectly. There will be times when you pray and still don't feel like you have anything constructive to say. How about in those times we just honestly admit that to our friends? In those times, don't put on the charade of super counselor. Instead reveal that you are weak, but he is strong. In relying on our own wisdom and strength, we think that being strong and wise will save, but it may be that God has determined that honesty and weakness is exactly what your friend needs to see.

Here is the really crazy good news—the Holy Spirit is strong enough to use all of your mess-ups, all of your failed attempts to help, all of your desire to take his place and be the Savior. He takes all of that and submits it to the will of the Father.

How can you love those who are unlovable? Pray for the help of the Holy Spirit. Pray that he will remind you of the truth and comfort you with the fact that you are loved beyond measure. Ask him to help you love in the face of opposition.

How can you love those who are in difficult circumstances? Pray for and seek after the help of the Holy Spirit. Pray he will remind you that it is not all up to you. Pray he will give you the right words to say or the ability to just be quiet. Pray he will teach you to depend more on his work.

Beloved, he is the Comforter, he is the Helper, he is the Counselor. May he use you and your brokenness to make his power appear as brilliant as it really is.

12

The Gospel for the Relationship Failure

So now we come to the end. You've read all about how God is your Father, Jesus is your brother and friend, and the Holy Spirit is your comforter and helper. We've explored the beautiful truth that Jesus is our High Priest and he sympathizes with us in our weaknesses. We've remembered that God is on mission to bring us to himself, and we've recalled that this mission includes the binding of broken hearts and the proclaiming of good news. We've fallen in love with our heavenly Husband all over again. We've seen how the God-Man came to earth to work and how he has redeemed our vocations forever. And now we are at the end.

You've got all the information you need to be the best friend, spouse, parent, churchgoer, employee, and child. You really understand this whole grace thing and how essential it is to your relationships. So now you and I won't fall into the same patterns of judgment and anger we have previously kept as bedfellows.

Or will we? I would like to declare that we are going to be free of all of our relational sin and brokenness, but the truth is that won't happen until we are perfected in our eternal home. For now we will struggle, we will fight to remember the gospel, and we will plead with the Holy Spirit to apply it to our lives. I often struggle with feeling condemnation because it seems like I should be better at this. After all, I wrote a book on relationships and am still bitter, envious, and angry to those around me. Where is there hope for those of us who continue to fail at relationships?

Paul and Barnabas

If there was one person, besides Jesus, in all of Scripture that you would say "got grace," who would it be? My immediate answer would be the apostle Paul! I mean, the man wrote the book of Romans, the greatest explanation of the gospel message and grace ever given, and also half of the New Testament. Paul was the grace superhero if there ever was one. And yet, because God is good and kind and loves us so very much, we have a remarkable story recorded in the book of Acts.

Paul and Barnabas have been the dynamic duo for the entirety of Acts up to chapter 15. They are traveling around the countryside, proclaiming the good news of forgiveness for sins and seeing large groups of people getting saved. They are brothers in the faith and brothers in ministry. Barnabas is Paul's right-hand man. Barnabas was one of the first people to welcome Paul into the group of believers after he was converted. He encouraged and helped Paul from the very beginning of his spiritual walk. They were inseparable. They did everything together and were the best of friends. On one of their trips together, they took along John Mark, who for some reason decided he didn't want to be on the trip anymore and went home. We don't read much about it, and it feels like an unimportant detail. And then we get to Acts 15:36–40 and read this:

> And after some days Paul said to Barnabas, "Let us return and visit the brothers in every city where we proclaimed the word of the Lord, and see how they are." Now Barnabas wanted to take with them John called Mark. But Paul thought best not to take with them one who had withdrawn from them in Pamphylia and had not gone with them to the work. And there arose a sharp disagreement, so that they separated from each other. Barnabas took Mark with him and sailed away to Cyprus, but Paul chose Silas and departed.

There's deep mystery to be uncovered here. Just from the minimal information we have, we see that Barnabas wants to bring along John Mark again, give him another shot, and extend grace to him, but Paul gets pretty worked up over it. He doesn't think they should bring John Mark. After all, he was the one who bailed before when it got a little difficult. It seems as though Paul is saying, "John Mark had his chance. Why would we give him another one?" Don't forget that this is Paul, the man who would eventually pen these words: "Let all bitterness and wrath and anger and clamor and slander be put away from you, along with all malice. Be kind to one another, tenderhearted, forgiving one another, as God in Christ forgave you" (Ephesians 4:31–32), and here he was seemingly withholding forgiveness. From our reading of the story, it doesn't seem that he was kind or tenderhearted toward John Mark at all. And then on top of that he gets in a "sharp disagreement" with Barnabas, his buddy. The words *sharp disagreement* don't mean some gentlemanly discussion with tea in hand; they got heated with each other and got in each other's faces. The Greek word is defined as "a severe argument based on intense difference of opinion—'sharp argument, sharp difference of opinion.'"[1] They were so upset with each other that they went in different directions. It was no small matter; it was probably a great source of pain and confusion for both Barnabas and Paul.

But the beautiful thing about the story is it doesn't end here. We don't know how or when they worked it out, but we do read in 2 Timothy 4:11 that Paul has these words to say about John Mark: "Get Mark and bring him with you, for he is very useful to me for ministry." Paul is now asking for the very same man he once dismissed. Not only does he ask for him, but he goes on to say that he is useful to him. God redeems. He takes sharp disagreements among brothers and turns them for his glory. On the day that Barnabas took Mark and sailed for Cyprus, he was probably pretty sure they wouldn't hear from Paul again, and if they did, he certainly wouldn't be asking for Mark to join him on another missionary trip!

The reconciliation that the gospel presents us with is a lovely thing to behold. Paul writes these words in 2 Corinthians 5:17–19:

> Therefore, if anyone is in Christ, he is a new creation. The old has passed away; behold, the new has come. All this is from God, who through Christ reconciled us to himself and gave us the ministry of reconciliation; that is, in Christ God was reconciling the world to himself, not counting their trespasses against them, and entrusting to us the message of reconciliation.

I wonder if when Paul wrote those words, he remembered his disagreement with Barnabas and Mark. Whether while he was scribbling down what the Holy Spirit ministered to his soul, he sat back and thought to himself, *What an astonishing God we serve. He reconciles us to himself, but that's not all—he also reconciles us to each other.*

The gospel, the power of God's forgiveness and love, is the only thing powerful enough to change this man's heart that was so set against Mark into one that asked for him. It reminds me of Paul's conversion. He hated Christians with a white-hot burning hatred, and yet Jesus came to him and asked why he was persecuting him. Jesus takes the haters like Paul and makes them into a people who love reconciliation. Paul wasn't perfect, and that gives me great hope when I fail in relationships. It helps me to know that even though there might be relationships I have hurt because of my own sin, that doesn't have to be the end of the story. Broken relationships will most likely need to involve seeking forgiveness and reconciliation, but I can give up on all of my "rights" and ask for forgiveness. I can also give up on my "rights" and seek reconciliation when I have been sinned against. No relationship is perfect, and even the apostle Paul had to deal with the tragedy of sin hurting others.

You may be in a relationship right now that you feel utter despair over. Your marriage could be ending, your children won't talk to you anymore, you have gossiped about a dear friend and she found out, your parents have written the word *failure* over your life, or maybe you've just had a huge fight with a co-worker. Again, hear these words of comfort and hope from 2 Corinthians: "Therefore, if anyone is in Christ, he is a new creation. The old has passed away; behold, the new has come" (v. 17). You are new. You don't have to be stuck in the way you previously responded to relationships, because the Holy Spirit promises to help you. Walk in the newness of life that has been given you:

All this is from God, who through Christ reconciled us to himself and gave us the ministry of reconciliation; that is, in Christ God was reconciling the world to himself, not counting their

197

trespasses against them, and entrusting to us the message of reconciliation.

vv. 18–19

This newness comes only from God, from the One who took rebels and changed them into beloved children. He knows what scalawags we are, and yet he gives us this same ministry of reconciliation. He doesn't count your past relational sins against you. He entrusts to you the message of reconciliation: "Therefore, we are ambassadors for Christ, God making his appeal through us" (v. 20). God makes his appeal to unbelievers through messed-up people like you and me. God makes his appeal to believers through relational failures like you and me.

"We implore you on behalf of Christ, be reconciled to God. For our sake he made him to be sin who knew no sin, so that in him we might become the righteousness of God" (vv. 20–21). And here is the kicker, the icing on the cake, the double rainbow, the fresh salsa on your warm tortilla chips: ALL of your sins in every relationship you have ever had have been placed on the Son. For you and for me Jesus Christ was made to be sin. Think of that specific relational sin that you feel might be the most unforgivable. Jesus Christ himself became that sin, for your sake! What glorious, heart-melting, earth-shattering, too-good-to-be-true news. And guess what! That's not all. He became sin so that we might become the righteousness of God. Think on that for just a minute. Don't rush past this. You, if you are hidden in Christ, are the *righteousness of God*. In every single way Jesus handled relationships perfectly; in every way he chose to love instead of hate; in every way he refused to demand his rights; and right now before the Father, you have that same righteousness. All the relationship righteousness he earned is now yours!

I Get Knocked Down

The fight of the Christian life is to believe that this is true. You and I are going to get knocked flat on our backsides in all of our relationships at one time or another. We just will. It is the reality of living in a sin-cursed world surrounded by sinners. We're going to sin against others and others will sin against us. But the good news of the gospel is that we can get up again by the grace of God. Not in our strength, not because we are superheroes, but because his grace is sufficient.

Do you feel like a relationship failure? As if you are too weak to ever get it right? Guess what? In that weakness, he will be strong. He will prove himself strong by forgiving you and loving you through it. He will prove himself strong by giving you the ability to love those you thought were unlovable. He will prove himself strong by taking the craziest, most wacked-out relationship in your life and turning it for his glory. And if he doesn't do those things, he is strong enough to sustain you in that difficulty. He will overwhelm you with his love in such a way that you will find yourself walking through a trial that you never expected to have the strength or courage to survive.

I have personally been involved in conflicts where I thought there was no way anything good would ever come of it. I can think of one time in particular where two parties had been going at it for months on end. I had had countless meetings with each party, tried to share gospel reconciliation, and was met over and over again with hardness and anger. When some other people got involved and we finally convinced them to meet, I thought punches might actually be thrown, and if they weren't, I was sure that awful, hurtful words would be. Before they arrived, I was sitting with my pastor and said sarcastically, "Well, the Holy Spirit better show up or we are going to have to call the police." He sort of laughed and said, "Well, I was planning on him being here." Sure enough, the meeting ended in tears and hugs and whispered confessions. I was undone. My lack of faith didn't stop God from working. He just stepped over me and got to work, and he allowed me to sit there with my mouth hanging open and watching. I walked away shaking my head in disbelief, asking myself, *What just happened?!* The gospel happened, the Holy Spirit happened, the ministry of reconciliation took place.

I have also seen situations where the result wasn't tied up with a pretty bow, where the hurt was too deep and the sin held too tightly. I have watched as families that were once incredibly close changed into virtual strangers. And I have thought, *How can this happen?* And yet Jesus has held these people close and reminded them of his great love. He has become their greatest treasure, and it is lovely to see.

The point is that Jesus takes it all and uses it for his glory. Every relationship, every failure, every brokenness is all redeemed by the blood of the Lamb. It may not be redeemed by reconciliation here on earth, but someday every tear will be wiped away. Most of the tears I have cried here on earth have been because of relational brokenness. All of those tears, every single one— the ones that were brought on because of my sin and the ones that were brought on because of the sin of others—will all be a distant memory when I see my Savior's face.

There will be no more sadness. We will intimately know that the very love we have looked for all of our lives has been ours the entire time. And instead of Christ looking at us and saying, "*See! I was here and you ignored me. Now I won't let you feel my love to the fullest,*" he will look at us and say, "*Well done, my good and faithful servant. Enter into my rest; enter into my love.*" We will finally see that we were home all along. He had us safely in the palm of his hand the entire time. We will rejoice with the angels because of the forgiveness we have received. We will sing great songs of joy because of the worthiness of the Lamb that was slain. The most hurtful and worst relationship will be a distant whisper from long ago, and his loving-kindness will fill our eyes and hearts.

Until that day, strive to live with that reality in view. Look at those with whom God has chosen to surround you and attempt to be tenderhearted, and kind, and love each other. And when you and I fail at that, we will look to his forgiveness that has been ours all along, and that will give us the strength to get back up again.

Until that day, pray that we will be marked by our love for each other. Pray that these words of Christ from John 13:35 will be true of us: "By this all people will know that you are my disciples, if you have love for one another." And on the days when it is true and we are given a special grace to love the way we have been loved, look to him and thank him profusely for allowing you to be a part of the ministry of reconciliation. And then, conversely, on the days that we are only known by our biting and devouring, may we run to 1 John 4, a chapter that talks all about how we ought to love each other, even going so far as to say that you can't say you love God and then hate your brother (v. 20). Look also at this hope-filled verse from 1 John 3: "For whenever our heart condemns us, God is greater than our heart, and he knows everything" (v. 20). He is greater than our hearts. He can change us. You don't need to feel condemned. Condemnation is a self-focus, while true godly sorrow leads you deeper into relationship with him: "But if anyone does sin, we have an advocate with the Father, Jesus Christ the righteous. He is the propitiation for our sins, and not for ours only but also for the sins of the whole world" (2:1–2).

When you sin in relationship, you have an advocate with the Father. You are free to confess your sins to God and to others.

You have nothing left to prove. You don't have to justify yourself anymore. He is your propitiation. He has taken away all of God's wrath. When you sin, you don't need to go into hiding; you are free to walk in the light with all of your failures exposed. He has already paid for them all.

Notes

Chapter 1: The Problem With Us

1. The word *karma* has a specific meaning in Hindu and Buddhist tradition in relation to a belief in reincarnation. *Merriam-Webster's Unabridged Dictionary* defines it as "the sum total of the ethical consequences of a person's good or bad actions comprising thoughts, words, and deeds that is held in Hinduism and Buddhism to determine his specific destiny in his next existence." However, in modern pop culture, the word has taken on a more general meaning of doing good in order to receive good in *this* life. This is how Earl means it, and it is what I mean by the word whenever I refer to it in this book.

Chapter 2: The Perfection of God

1. Matthew Henry, *Matthew Henry's Commentary on the Whole Bible: Complete and Unabridged in One Volume* (Peabody, MA: Hendrickson, 1994), 1621.

2. Martyn Lloyd-Jones, *Fellowship With God* (Wheaton, IL: Crossway, 2012), 63.

3. Jady Koch, *The Mockingbird Devotional: Good News for Today (and Every Day)* (Charlottesville, VA: Mockingbird Ministries, 2013), 34.

4. Donald McAllister, "Spurgeon's 'The King and the Carrot' (Why Religious Change Doesn't Work)," http://donaldmcallister.com/carrot.

5. *Luther's Small Catechism with Explanation* (St. Louis: Concordia Publishing House, 1991), Explanation #77, 173.

Chapter 3: How Do We Change?

1. William Arndt, Frederick W. Danker, and Walter Bauer, *A Greek-English Lexicon of the New Testament and Other Early Christian Literature* (Chicago: University of Chicago Press, 2000), 7.

2. Thomas Chalmers, "The Expulsive Power of a New Affection," *Manna Christian Fellowship*, http://manna.mycpanel.princeton.edu/rubberdoc/c8618ef3f4a7b5424f710c5fb61ef281.pdf.

Chapter 4: God Our Father and Our Relationships With Our Children

1. J.I. Packer, *Knowing God* (Great Britain: InterVarsity Press, 1973), 188.
2. Ibid., 201.
3. Elyse M. Fitzpatrick and Jessica Thompson, *Give Them Grace* (Wheaton, IL: Crossway, 2011), 55.

Chapter 5: Jesus Our Friend and Our Friendships

1. D. A. Carson, *The Gospel According to John (The Pillar New Testament Commentary)* (Leicester, England; Grand Rapids, MI: InterVarsity Press; Eerdmans, 1991), 522.
2. Scotty Smith, *Gospel Transformation Study Bible* (Wheaton, IL: Crossway, 2013), Notes on John, 1436.
3. Matthew Henry, *Matthew Henry's Commentary on the Whole Bible: Complete and Unabridged in One Volume* (Peabody, MA: Hendrickson, 1994), 2019.
4. C.S. Lewis, *The Four Loves: An Exploration of the Nature of Love* (New York: Harcourt Brace, 1960), 121.
5. Ibid., 8.
6. Henri J.M. Nouwen, *Out of Solitude: Three Meditations on the Christian Life* (Notre Dame, IN: Ave Maria Press, 2004), 38.
7. Octavius Winslow, "Consider Jesus—as Receiving Sinners," *Grace Gems*, www.gracegems.org/Winslows/consider_jesus28.htm.

Chapter 6: God's Mission and Our Relationships With Our Communities

1. Penn Jillette, "Not proselytize," *YouTube*, www.youtube.com/watch?v=ow Zc3Xq8obk&index=2&list=PLe1QpNNS5GeUczkTNkLqKqcMOwJYgWxJt.
2. C.H. Spurgeon, "Our Lord's Preaching," February 16, 1911, www.spurgeon gems.org/vols55-57/chs3237.pdf.
3. Octavius Winslow, *The Inner Life*, 1850, *Grace Gems*, www.gracegems.org /WINSLOW/The%20Broken%20and%20Contrite%20Heart.htm.
4. Octavius Winslow, "The Sympathy of Christ," *Grace Gems*, www.gracegems .org/WINSLOW/The%20Tears%20of%20Christ.htm.

Chapter 7: God Our Husband and Our Marriages

1. *ESV Gospel Transformation Bible* (Wheaton, IL: Crossway, 2013), notes on 2 Cor. 11:1–6, 1566, emphasis mine.
2. Charles H. Spurgeon, *Morning and Evening: Daily Readings, Complete and Unabridged* (Peabody, MA: Hendrickson, 2006), March 20, Evening.
3. Tullian Tchividjian, *One Way Love: Inexhaustible Grace for an Exhausted World* (Colorado Springs: David C. Cook, 2013), 151, emphasis mine.
4. Ibid., 157.

Chapter 8: Jesus Our Brother and Our Relationships
With Our Families

1. Charles Spurgeon, "The Joint Heirs and Their Divine Portion," Sermon delivered July 28, 1861, *The Spurgeon Archive*, www.spurgeon.org/sermons/0402.htm.

2. J.I. Packer, *Knowing God*, 258.

3. Sammy Rhodes, "Parent Wounds," *Embracing Awkward*, April 1, 2014, http://sammyrhodes.co/embracingawkward/14007365.

4. Timothy Lane and Paul David Tripp, *Relationships: A Mess Worth Making* (Greensboro, NC: New Growth Press, 2008), 13.

Chapter 9: Jesus Our High Priest and Our Relationships
With Church Members

1. Ken Sande, "The High Cost of Conflict Among Christians," Peacemaker Ministries, http://www.peacemaker.net/site/c.aqKFLTOBIpH/b.1320145/k.23DE /The_High_Cost_of_Conflict_Among_Christians.htm#4.

2. Ibid.

3. *New City Catechism,* adapted by Timothy Keller and Sam Shammas from the Reformation catechisms (CreateSpace, 2012), 100.

4. *ESV Gospel Transformation Bible* (Wheaton, IL: Crossway, 2013), notes on Exodus 28:1–43, 112.

5. Ibid.

6. *ESV Gospel Transformation Bible*, notes on John 18:15–18, 25–27, 1441.

7. Elyse M. Fitzpatrick, *Found in Him* (Wheaton, IL: Crossway, 2013), 44.

8. John Piper, "Draw Near to the Throne of Grace with Confidence," sermon preached at Bethlehem Baptist Church, September 15, 1996, www.desiringgod. org/sermons/draw-near-to-the-throne-of-grace-with-confidence.

9. C.H. Spurgeon, "The Tenderness of Jesus," No. 2148, sermon delivered June 8, 1890, at The Metropolitan Tabernacle, Newington, www.spurgeongems.org/vols34-36/ chs2148.pdf.

10. Octavius Winslow, "Consider Jesus—as Tempted by Satan," *Grace Gems*, www.gracegems.org/Winslows/consider_jesus12.htm, emphasis Spurgeon's.

11. John MacDuff, "Christ the Intercessor," http://gracegems.org/MacDuff1/r13.htm.

12. Sinclair Ferguson, *Children of the Living God* (Carlisle, PA: Banner of Truth, 1989).

13. Octavius Winslow, "The Sympathy of Christ," *Grace Gems*, www.gracegems .org/WINSLOW/The%20Emotion%20of%20Anger%20in%20Christ.htm.

14. C.H. Spurgeon, "The Tenderness of Jesus."

15. Paul E. Miller, *A Loving Life* (Wheaton, IL: Crossway, 2014), 30.

16. Tim Keller uses a phrase similar to this in his writings and preaching.

Chapter 10: Jesus a Carpenter and Our Relationships
With Our Co-Workers

1. Elyse Fitzpatrick, *Found in Him*, 60.

2. Klaus Issler, "Jesus at Work," *Biola Magazine,* Summer 2012, http://magazine. biola.edu/article/12-summer/jesus-at-work.

3. Martin Luther, *Exposition of Psalm 147*, quoted by Gustaf Wingren, *Luther on Vocation* (Evansville, IN: Ballast Press, 1994), 137–138.

Chapter 11: The Holy Spirit Our Comforter/Helper and Our Relationships With Difficult People

1. Francis Chan, *The Forgotten God: Reversing Our Tragic Neglect of the Holy Spirit* (Colorado Springs: David C. Cook, 2009), 19.

2. Johannes P. Louw and Eugene Albert Nida, *Greek-English Lexicon of the New Testament: Based on Semantic Domains* (New York: United Bible Societies, 1996), 141.

3. M. G. Easton, *Easton's Bible Dictionary* (New York: Harper & Brothers, 1893), 38.

4. *The Westminster Confession of Faith* (Lawrenceville, GA: Christian Education and Publications, 2005), 10.

5. Ibid.

6. Abraham Kuyper, *The Work of the Holy Spirit* (Grand Rapids, MI: Eerdmans, 1975), 524.

Chapter 12: The Gospel for the Relationship Failure

1. Johannes P. Louw and Eugene Albert Nida, *Greek-English Lexicon of the New Testament: Based on Semantic Domains* (New York: United Bible Societies, 1996), 439.

Jessica Thompson grew up in Southern California, the second child of Phil and Elyse Fitzpatrick. After graduation from high school, she completed a bachelor's degree in theology and married Cody Thompson. The Lord has blessed Cody and Jessica with three children: Wesley, Hayden, and Allie. Together they serve at Westview Church, an Acts 29 church plant in north San Diego County. When not homeschooling, Jessica is a regular speaker at conferences.

Jessica and Elyse have collaborated on the books *Give Them Grace: Dazzling Your Kids with the Love of Jesus* and *Answering Your Kids' Toughest Questions*.